DIRECTIONS IN DEVELOPMENT

Early Child Development

Investing in the Future

The World Bank
Washington, D.C.

1818 H Street, NW
Washington, D.C. 20433

Manufactured in the United States of America
First printing January 1996

The findings, interpretations, and conclusions expressed in this study are entirely those of the authors and should not be attributed in any manner to the World Bank, to its affiliated organizations, or to members of its Board of Executive Directors or the countries they represent.

ISBN 0-8213-3547-2

Photos: Cover, Jean-Luc Ray, Aga Khan Foundation; pages 7, 17, 19, 34, 36, 41, 48, 82, Jean-Luc Ray, Aga Khan Foundation; page 79, Curt Carnemark, World Bank.

Library of Congress Cataloging-in-Publication Data

Young, Mary Eming, 1955–
Early child development : investing in the future.
p. cm. — (Directions in development)
Includes bibliographical references.
ISBN 0-8213-3547-2
1. Economic development—Effect of education on. 2. Child development. 3. Early childhood education. I. Title II. Series : Directions in development (Washington, D.C.).
HD75.7.Y68 1996
372.21—dc20 96-53256
CIP

Contents

Foreword

The past four decades have seen unprecedented progress in health and education in developing countries. Much of this progress is associated with economic growth and the resulting improvement in living conditions. But despite tremendous progress on average, many countries—and within countries, many population groups—have failed to benefit. Every year more than 11 million children die from preventable diseases, and 130 million children—most of them girls—do not attend primary school. The students who will enter primary school in the year 2000 have already been born and are even now being prepared for their future lives. What happens to them in this stage of their lives will in large part determine the course of the coming millennium.

Children whose earliest years are blighted by hunger or disease or whose minds are not stimulated by appropriate interaction with adults and their environment pay for these early deficits throughout their lives—and so does society. Such children are far more likely than their more fortunate peers to do poorly in school, to drop out early, to be functionally illiterate, and to be only marginally employable in today's increasingly high-technology world. Collectively, these children who have been deprived in early life therefore affect labor productivity and national economic prosperity.

Yet none of this need happen. Early childhood programs have been shown to enhance school readiness, increase the efficacy of investments in primary schools and human capital formation, foster beneficial social behavior and thereby lessen social welfare costs, and promote community development. Moreover, child care arrangements that provide safe havens for preschoolers during the day allow mothers to join the workforce, with benefits for all members of the family.

Programs that remedy critical early childhood deficiencies are therefore fundamental—not only to the success of each child in life, but also to the success of society as a whole. It is not surprising that policymakers and parents alike have now joined health, education, and nutrition specialists in acknowledging the importance of integrated early childhood interventions—programs designed to improve children's health and nutrition and to stimulate their minds from their earliest years.

Health and education projects are central to the World Bank's strategy of poverty reduction, and the Bank has directed significant investment toward young children—the human capital of the future. Improved immunizations, basic health care, prenatal care, and nutrition services provided by Bank-supported programs have helped to reduce child mortality rates dramatically in developing countries. But to help stimulate the minds of the world's children and prepare them for a healthy and productive life, much more can and must be done.

The World Bank's chief goal is to reduce poverty, and it has regarded economic growth as the chief engine for achieving that goal. Thus, throughout its fifty years the Bank has directed both money and expertise to countries striving to achieve macroeconomic stability, an open economy, access to world markets, incentive structures that promote investment, functioning capital and labor markets, and the host of other reforms that spur economic growth.

But since the 1980s the World Bank has opened a new front in its fight against poverty by tripling its lending for health, education, nutrition, reproductive health, and other aspects of human capital development. The Bank's social service lending now averages more than US$3 billion a year—substantially more than goes to support programs of economic reform—making the Bank the largest supporter of social programs in the world.

To improve the lives of the women and children who make up the majority of the world's poor, the Bank has given special attention to efforts that improve the quality and reach of basic services in health and education. To achieve better results with these efforts, it is increasingly joining forces with the many nongovernmental organizations that have long worked in areas neglected by the formal service network.

Between 1990 and 1995 the Bank lent US$5.9 billion—about a third of its social sector lending for that period—for projects in health and education that would benefit children directly. These projects were both freestanding and incorporated in broad social sector efforts. Over the coming decade the Bank's social lending is slated to rise further, which should substantially help countries' efforts to improve the lives of their children.

This report offers the reader an overview of the many programs around the world that are targeting children from birth to the age of eight. These programs are supported and run by national governments, multinational organizations, bilateral donors, and a host of nongovernmental organizations. As part of the Bank's Directions in Development series, this report complements such other reports as *Enriching Lives,* an up-to-date summary of cost-effective investments in micronutrients; *Building Human Capital for Better Lives,* which focuses on strategies for building human capital within a sound macroeconomic environment; *Investing in People,* which highlights successful Bank-supported efforts across the social sector spectrum; and *Private and Public Initiatives,* which explores a variety of methods that governments and private entrepreneurs around the world have developed to bring basic services to the people.

The second half of the report briefly describes a variety of early child development programs now in operation. Policymakers and program managers may find these sketches useful when designing programs for preschool children. No matter the country or cultural setting of such programs, they share a single goal: improving very young children's development and therefore their prospects for the future.

To achieve this goal, some projects concentrate on educating caregivers, others on delivering services directly to the children. Still others seek to inform the public about the need for such projects in order to increase demand or about ways to improve the quality of parental care. Early childhood interventions use home visits, parental and teacher training, center-based care, educational radio and television shows, and a host of other methods to carry out these varied purposes.

Many of the programs described here are still too new to have established a track record, but are included, along with programs tested and proved over the years, to present the full range of possibilities. This concise outline of theory, proven results, and present practice in early child development is offered with the aim of showing the world development community how investment in young children can help break the vicious intergenerational cycle of poverty in the developing world.

Armeane M. Choksi
Vice President
Human Capital Development and Operations Policy

Acknowledgments

This report benefited from the contributions of many people. Jacques van der Gaag advised me from the beginning on the content and form of the report. My sincerest thanks are due to colleagues from outside the Bank for their contributions: Carrie Auer (Save the Children Foundation), Kathy Bartlett (Aga Khan Foundation), Jay Belsky (Pennsylvania State University), John Bennett (UNESCO), Netta Ben-Porath Bruno and Avima Lombard (Hebrew University), Judith Evans, Ellen Ilfeld, and Robert Myers (Consultative Group on Early Childhood Care and Development), Cigdem Kagitcibasi (University of Turkey), Robert LeVine (Harvard University), Beryl Levinger (Academy for Educational Development), Ricardo Moran (Inter-American Development Bank), Kate Torkington (Bernard van Leer Foundation), Kate Walsh (Children's Resources International), David Weikart (High/Scope Educational Research Foundation), and Fred Wood (Save the Children). I have drawn liberally from their work and benefited from their suggestions. Special thanks go to Margaret Kajeckas, who helped prepare the country cases, and to Elizabeth Sherman, who worked with me from the beginning as writer and editor. Within the Bank, Martha Ainsworth, Jayshree Balachander, Jacques Baudouy, Lloyd Briggs, Bruce Carlson, Mariam Claeson, Joy Del Rosso, Marito Garcia, Betty Hanan, Stephen Heyneman, Althea Hill, Nuria Homedes, Robin Horn, Arun Joshi, Federico Joubert, David Klaus, Karen Lashman, Frans Lenglet, Antonio Lim, Judith McGuire, Eileen Nkwanga, Philip B. Okeefe, Juan Prawda, Joel Reyes, Miriam Schneidman, James Socknat, and Jane Thomas all contributed written materials and useful commentary. Because of the dedication in the field of Bank operations staff, whose work is reflected in part II of this report, I was able to showcase a wide variety of innovative early child development programs in the developing world. Preparation of the report was managed by Euna Osbourne of the Human Development Department. Heather Imboden and Christian Perez of American Writing Corporation laid out the text. Finally, the preparation and publication of this booklet were financed by the Norwegian Trust Fund. Many thanks to all of you.

PART I

The Theory

The Case for Early Intervention

A child's experiences in the first months and years of life determine whether he or she will enter school eager to learn or not. By school age, family and caregivers have already prepared the child for success or failure. The community has already helped or hindered the family's capacity to nurture the child's development.

– Dr. T. Barry Brazelton, Children's Hospital Medical Center, Boston, Massachusetts (as quoted in Bernard van Leer Foundation 1994, p. 13)

With twelve of thirteen infants now surviving to age one, the number of children in the developing world—where four-fifths of all children live—is burgeoning (Myers 1995). Until recently, facing staggering infant mortality rates, poor countries were forced to concentrate their meager resources on ensuring their children's survival and had to largely ignore the less immediate problem of how to enrich their future prospects.

As a result, in developing countries today it is estimated that only 1 percent of mothers get help beyond that provided by family and friends in rearing their infants; only 1 percent of eligible Sub-Saharan children are enrolled in preschool programs; and few developing countries have achieved preschool coverage of even 25 to 30 percent. By contrast, 80 percent of three-year-olds in Belgium, Denmark, France, and Italy are enrolled in nursery or preschool centers (Bennett 1993).

Yet at the same time, ever more women are entering the workforce, and ever more households are headed by women alone. This demographic shift is being experienced from Eastern Europe to Latin America and from Africa to the United States. And where both parents or the only parent works, access to affordable, high-quality child care becomes an economic necessity as well as a social one.

For it is well documented that integrated programs in early child development can do much to prevent malnutrition, stunted cognitive development, and insufficient preparation for school. Thirty years of research have shown that such programs can improve primary and even secondary school performance, increase children's prospects for higher productivity and future income, and reduce the probability that they will become burdens on public health and social service budgets.

Interventions early in children's lives can also raise mothers' status in the home and community, help to reduce gender inequity, increase women's participation in the labor force, and increase community participation in development efforts.

What, then, makes an early child development program good? A basic requirement is that it keep children healthy and secure. In the areas of mental stimulation and education, we still have much to learn.

A quarter-century of U.S. preschool research has identified several features that successful, center-based preschool programs share. Yet some of these features—such as a staff ratio of two adults for a group of twenty children—require lavish resources and cannot be reproduced in developing countries. (In Kenya, for instance, that ratio is nearer to 1:70 than 1:10.) But both research and experience have taught us that many principles of early education are universal. The idea of exploratory play as the best teaching tool, for instance, is just as useful to mothers tending their own or neighborhood children in their homes as to paid teachers in established day care centers. Thus the Western studies detailed here are presented not so much as models to be imitated but as examples of "best practice" with much to offer anyone interested in helping young children learn.

This booklet is intended for practitioners in the field already working in early child development or just beginning to address it in their work. It takes an inventory of what we know about the reasons for investing in early child development, about the elements of quality early child interventions, and about complementary program options being implemented by governments, nongovernmental organizations (NGOs), and multilateral and bilateral donors. Some questions whose answers would help guide program design remain unresolved—such as the relative merit and the effects of formal and nonformal child development services in different country conditions, the comparative costs of programs ranging from formal to nonformal to parental education, and appropriate roles for government, the private sector, and NGOs in financing early child interventions. And we still know little, for instance, about fathers' role in early education programs. Their participation and their families' is certainly needed. But how to engage them remains to be studied.

Scientific Basis

The effects of health care, nutrition, and mental stimulation on children's mental and emotional growth—as reflected in their ability to master ever more complex activities—and physical growth are synergistic and cannot be broken up into separate domains. Integrated programs therefore seek to address all of children's basic needs. In addition to food, protection, and health care, child care programs must also provide affection, intellectual stimulation, supportive human interaction, and opportunities and activities that promote learning.

Studies conducted in the United States during the 1960s to the mid-1970s confirmed that intervention early in a child's life has lasting positive effects. With the basic question of long-term efficacy resolved, a second wave of studies was free to investigate the effects produced by different program models. Current research in the field seeks to build on these findings, to identify more precisely what makes small-scale programs effective, and to devise ways to expand them to a national scale (Mitchell, Weiss, and Schultz 1992).

The crucial early years. Medical and educational research have both shown that mental growth—that is, the development of intelligence, personality, and social behavior—occurs most rapidly in humans during their earliest years. It is estimated, in fact, that half of all intellectual development potential is established by age four (Bloom 1964). It is also now known that the brain responds most to very early experience, and brain research has documented the environment's effect on brain function. Because of the importance of the early years, intervention even in kindergarten may be too late to help develop young children's capacities. By contrast, the effectiveness of quality early child development programs in spurring children's mental, emotional, and physical development has been documented by the past thirty years of research.

According to the Carnegie Task Force on Meeting the Needs of Young Children (1994):

- Brain development before age one is more rapid and extensive than was previously realized. Although cell formation is virtually complete before birth, brain maturation continues after birth.
- Brain development is much more vulnerable to environmental influence than was suspected. Inadequate nutrition before birth and in the first years of life can seriously interfere with brain development and lead to such neurological and behavioral disorders as learning disabilities and mental retardation.
- The influence of early environment on brain development is long-lasting. There is considerable evidence showing that infants exposed to good nutrition, toys, and playmates had measurably better brain function at twelve years of age than those raised in a less stimulating environment.
- Environment affects not only the number of brain cells and the number of connections among them but also the way these connections are "wired." The process of eliminating excess neurons and synapses from the dense, immature brain, which continues well into adolescence, is most dramatic in the early years of life, and it is guided to a large extent by the child's sensory experience of the outside world.
- Early stress can affect brain function, learning, and memory adversely and permanently. New research provides a scientific basis for the long-recognized fact that children who experience extreme stress in their earliest years are at greater risk for developing a variety of cognitive, behavioral, and emotional difficulties later in life.

Box 1 Five reasons to invest in young children

To build human resources in a scientifically proven manner. Research has shown that half of a person's intelligence potential is developed by age four and that early childhood interventions can have a lasting effect on intellectual capacity, personality, and social behavior. Integrated programs that target children in their very early years are therefore critical for their mental and psychosocial development.

To generate higher economic returns and reduce social costs. By increasing children's desire and ability to learn, investment in early child education can increase the return on investment in their later education by making that education more effective. It can also enable participants to earn more and can raise their productivity in the workforce. Early investment in children can reduce the need for public welfare expenditures later and cut down on the social and financial costs associated with grade repetition, juvenile delinquency, and drug use.

To achieve greater social equity. Integrated programs for young children can modify the effects of socioeconomic and gender-related inequities, some of the most entrenched causes of poverty. Studies from diverse cultures show that girls enrolled in early childhood programs are better prepared for school and frequently stay in school longer. Early childhood interventions also free older sisters from the task of tending preschoolers, so that they can to return to school.

To increase the efficacy of other investments. Including early childhood interventions in larger programs can enhance the programs' efficacy. Early childhood interventions in health and nutrition programs increase children's chances of survival. Interventions in education programs prepare children for school, improving their performance and reducing the need for repetition.

To help mothers as well as children. With ever more mothers working and more households headed by women, safe child care has become a necessity. Providing safe child care allows women the chance to continue their education and learn new skills.

Helping parents meet their children's changing developmental needs. The younger the child, the more difficult it is to identify precisely which physiological and psychological factors govern health, and children's needs in these areas change as they progress from infancy to toddlerhood to preschool to primary school.

As a child becomes a toddler, for instance, most important is to provide a safe, clean environment and proper food. But because feeding is an interactive as well as a physical process, even so straightforward a need as nutrition has psychological aspects. Lack of proper handling and affection has been shown to cause children's growth to falter just as much as lack of proper food.

Parents, especially those who are young and inexperienced, are too often unaware of the fundamental needs of a young child and of the

many simple ways available to meet them. Many get their first lessons in constructive child care through early child development programs.

By the same token, only with whole-hearted parental participation can such programs succeed. Both studies and field experience have shown that parental involvement in preschool programs, for instance, results in more and more timely school enrollments and better attendance rates overall. Not surprisingly, therefore, where both parents and infants are targeted—as in Colombia's Programa para el Mejoramiento de la Educación, la Salud, y el Ambienta (Promesa) and in Haryana, India—dropout rates have declined dramatically. Parental involvement appears to be essential, moreover, if gains from preschool interventions are to be sustained.

Socioeconomic Returns

By increasing early abilities, preschool programs increase both the prospective earnings potential from a given level of schooling and the net prospective benefits from additional schooling. Several U.S. studies have confirmed preschool programs' efficacy as a means to increase the return to primary and secondary school investments, contribute to human capital formation, raise participants' productivity and income levels, and—by lowering health, welfare, and education costs—reduce public expenditures. Even a few years of early schooling, it appears, can substantially increase the economic value of an individual's skills (Selowsky 1981; Psacharopoulos 1986).

The evidence. A review of seventy-one reports on U.S. Head Start preschool programs found evidence of positive effects on IQ, better-developed abilities at the point of entry into school (school readiness), and greater achievement at the end of the early grades (Schweinhart 1992). Seven other long-term studies in the United States confirmed that

Box 2 UNICEF in Peru: the Wawa Wasi home child care program

Quality day care for young children is desperately needed in Peru, where more than half of families earn too little to cover their basic needs and 37 percent of working women are gone from the home ten hours a day. Yet as it now stands, child care services reach only a quarter of Peru's four-year-olds and just three of every 200 children under age three.

In 1993, therefore, the Ministry of Education and UNICEF initiated a plan to design, start, and regulate Wawa Wasi—a national home day care system that would work in conjunction with the National Food Aid Program. The system, coordinated jointly by the government and UNICEF, is designed and operated by government ministries, the National Family Welfare Institute, churches, and a confederation of grass-roots organizations.

Located in urban shantytowns, Wawa Wasi sets up a "community educational home" in the house of a local woman who is designated as the community's caregiver and trained in health care, early stimulation, and basic nutrition. For a small fee, working mothers may leave all children under the age of three with the caregiver. Mothers using the Wawa Wasi services also organize into parents associations and are expected to try to involve other family members.

Meals for the children are arranged through communal kitchens, "Glass of Milk" committees, or other food aid programs. The 280 communal kitchens now serving roughly ten Wawa Wasi educational homes each, however, were originally set up to prepare food for adults and must be trained to make nutritious meals for children. Each day care home receives basic equipment—mattresses, water cylinders, tables, chairs, and toys—and, if needed, a loan to repair or install lavatories. Nearby schools often collect and recycle materials for toys, mobiles, and other items useful to the young children.

Wawa Wasi has established 5,500 community educational homes and provided roughly 700,000 children under the age of six with integrated care. It has also extended the coverage of nonformal preschool education programs (Pronoeis) by 10 percent. Successfully mobilizing community interest and resources, it has signed agreements to provide for the needs of preschoolers in forty-eight provinces. It has distributed material on maternal survival and child development, produced and donated by Peruvian Education Facts for Life, to an estimated 2 million poor women. And it has coordinated government, private, grassroots, and family efforts in a way that is promising for the program's enduring success.

Source: UNICEF 1995, p. 21.

educational child care programs for youngsters living in poverty have the potential to confer important long-term benefits. Parents' involvement in educating their children was also shown to be critical to the lasting success of Head Start (Zigler and Muenchow 1992).

The U.S.-based Abecedarian Study—replicated in Project CARE and in the Infant Health and Development Program—consistently found that the most vulnerable young children were also the most positively affected by high-quality early intervention.

The Infant Health and Development Program was an eight-site, randomized, controlled trial of the efficacy of educational techniques developed in the preschool segments of the Abecedarian and CARE experiments. Most of the 985 low-birth-weight infants who participated were born to socially and economically disadvantaged mothers. Under the program, intensive early intervention was shown to prevent developmental delay. When compared with randomized controls, the incidence of mental retardation (that is, of IQs measured at less than 70) was reduced by an average factor of 2.7 (Ramey and others 1990). The stimulation program was started as early as three months of age, while in other programs it was started at about three years of age (Campbell and Ramey 1994).

Similar studies in Asia, the Middle East, and Latin America confirmed that early intervention can increase school readiness, promote timely school enrollment, lower repetition and dropout rates, and improve academic skills. R. G. Myers's (1995) review of nineteen longitudinal evaluations of the effect of early intervention in Latin America found that participating children were far less likely to have to repeat grades in primary school. The following benefits have been firmly linked to integrated interventions in early childhood:

- *Improved nutrition and health.* By providing psychosocial stimulation, early child development programs can enhance the efficacy of health care and nutrition initiatives. They can also help ensure that children receive health care. Children participating in the Colombia Community Child Care and Nutrition Project and the Bolivia Integrated Child Development projects, for instance, are required to complete their immunizations within six months of entering. Programs can also monitor growth and provide food supplements and micronutrients and can help with such existing public health efforts as mass immunizations.
- *Higher intelligence.* Children who participated in early child interventions under Jamaica's first Home Visiting Program, Colombia's Cali project, Peru's Programa No Formal de Educación Inicial (Pronoei), and the Turkey Early Enrichment Project scored higher, on average, on intellectual aptitude tests than did nonparticipants.
- *Higher school enrollment.* The Colombia Promesa program cited significantly higher enrollment rates among program children than among nonparticipants.

Box 3 Who is caring for the children in Eastern Europe?

In post-communist Bulgaria, Hungary, Poland, and Romania social services once provided by the state—such as comprehensive maternity benefits, maternity cash grants, monthly child allowances, liberal parental leave (including paid leave to care for sick children), housing subsidies for families with children, and crèches and kindergartens—are being progressively pared away. State-run enterprises are divesting themselves of the nonprofitmaking responsibility of providing child care for workers. National governments have shifted responsibility for such services to local authorities, who are poorer and less well equipped to supply them at the same level of quality. Local governments are introducing user fees to help defray expenses. And yet even as state-run child care facilities are being closed or priced out of reach, more mothers of young children are forced to go to work. Because families cannot survive on a single wage, in Bulgaria, for instance, 20 percent of working women hold two jobs. Who, then, is minding the children?

Expectations
At its best the old system of state-supported child care centers provided appropriate, high-quality care—including mental stimulation activities, health care, and three to five meals a day. Yet even so, many mothers, supported by state grants, chose to stay home with their infants. In the four countries studied, crèche enrollments never exceeded 14 percent of the age group, and enrollment rates were even lower in other communist countries. But kindergartens for children aged three to seven, with a 170-year tradition in Eastern Europe, were widely used.

Present-day realities
All of the countries studied (except Romania) have decentralized the responsibility for social services and cut family support services. Only provisions for parental leave have been left intact, or even strengthened, with the idea of promoting home-based child care. And more young women than ever are now out of work, for private businesses seeking to avoid paying maternity benefits either put young women on short-term contracts or do not hire them at all.

Box 3 continues on the next page

- *Less repetition.* Children who participated in an early childhood program repeated fewer grades and made better progress through school than did nonparticipants in similar circumstances. Children in the Colombia Promesa study, in the Alagoas and Fortaleza study in Northeast Brazil, and in the Argentina study all had, on average, lower rates of repetition.
- *Fewer dropouts.* Dropout rates were lower for program children in three of four studies. In the India Dalmau program—the only study in which attendance was measured—attendance rose by 16 percent for program children between the ages of six and eight. In the Colombia

Box 3, continued

Despite young families' desperate need for income, 70 percent of unemployed women in Bulgaria are under the age of thirty (UNICEF 1994). Thus, most of Eastern Europe's youngest children today spend their earliest years at home with their mothers or with extended family. But in many of these homes, incomes, housing, and even food supplies are insufficient and unpredictable.

Over the past decade, the region's birth rate has dropped. Although the percentage of children attending kindergartens has not yet changed dramatically, enrollments are declining. Of the countries studied, all but Poland had more preschool places available than children seeking them. Without state funding, the quality of center-based care is also declining. And as user fees put child care centers out of poor parents' reach, new issues of equity are coming to the fore.

What can be done

- *Explore alternative forms of child care.* With center-based care's accessibility and quality in question, Eastern Europeans today need to seek ways to strengthen family- and community-based child care.
- *Invest in materials and classes to educate parents.* Parents who grew up under a state-centered approach need to learn the techniques and practices best suited to home-based care.
- *Support nongovernmental organizations.* NGOs, emerging as important actors in the social service sector, need financial support and training to devise and implement new family service models.
- *Monitor the effects of government policy.* Monitoring systems and studies are needed to determine the impact of economic and social policy changes and to plan the most effective response.
- *Focus policymakers' attention on early child development.* Policymakers need to seek ways to keep early childhood interventions—which benefit the whole society—widely accessible and to keep standards uniform and high.

Source: Evans 1995.

Promesa project, third-grade enrollment rates rose by 100 percent, reflecting lower dropout and repetition rates. Moreover, 60 percent of program children reached the fourth grade, compared with only 30 percent of the comparison group.

Help for the disadvantaged. There is mounting evidence that interventions in early childhood particularly benefit the poor and disadvantaged. In India's Haryana project, for instance, dropout rates did not change significantly for children from the higher caste but fell a dramatic 46 percent for the lower caste and an astonishing 80 percent for the middle caste (Chaturvedi and others 1987). The Jamaica study gives unequivocal proof that nutritional supplementation for undernourished children—

who are most likely to come from disadvantaged families—improves mental development (Grantham-McGregor and others 1991). A program in Argentina was especially successful in lowering the enrollment ages of rural and low-income groups, while in Indian and Guatemalan programs, enrollment ages only declined significantly for another traditionally disadvantaged group—girls (Myers 1995).

Girls derive considerable benefit from early childhood interventions, for the barrier of gender inequality frequently affects them even before they enter school. In many African countries fewer than half as many girls as boys are enrolled in primary school. Studies from diverse cultures show that girls who participate in early child interventions are better prepared for and more likely to attend school. And where girls' success in school changes parents' expectations, many are allowed to continue their education.

Achieving gender equity in education is now known to be economically as well as ethically desirable. Educated women have fewer children and take better care of them. Mother's level of schooling is a better predictor of a child's cognitive growth, health, and reproductive outcomes than are family income, breadwinner's occupation, or other household variables.

Early interventions targeting girls reduce maternal fertility and infant and child mortality rates. Expanding girls' school enrollment therefore offers developing countries a cost-effective way to improve life expectancy and health and control fertility (LeVine and others 1994).

Investment in education associated with early stimulation and sensory-motor readiness yields a far higher rate of return than does equal investment in secondary or higher education (Psacharopoulos 1986). In the High/Scope Perry Preschool Program initiated in 1962, for instance, an investment of US$1.00 was estimated to yield US$7.16 in savings from lower education and welfare expenditures combined with gains in productivity (Schweinhart, Barnes, and Weikart 1993). Such a cost-benefit ratio may be overestimated if applied to developing countries, however, because it includes benefit outcomes (such as lower welfare expenditures) that developing countries simply do not have.

Policy Implications

Integrated early child development programs may be the single most effective intervention for helping poor children, families, communities, and nations break the intergenerational cycle of poverty. But to be successful and sustainable, such programs must be an integral part of countries' overall strategy for developing human capital.

National governments—while not necessarily directly involved in service delivery—are generally responsible for setting and maintaining child education standards. Kenya's Ministry of Education, for instance, registers, inspects, and supervises preschool sites; develops curriculums;

advises program administrators; formulates policy guidelines; and trains teachers and supervisors. Kenya has also established a National Center for Early Childhood Education to coordinate the development of training programs, provide a national support system, and evaluate local programs.

Peru and India are among the few developing countries that have established a national policy on early child education. Peru's 1972 education reform extended the responsibility of the Ministry of Education downward to children below age five. The ministry established preschools and began experimenting with parental education programs, and supported occasional local initiatives involving center-based child care and community volunteers. Under India's national policy for children (in place since 1975), the National Children's Board was established to coordinate the delivery of child services.

Although the scope and content of a child development policy will vary with the needs and resources of each country, certain program goals are recognized as universal: giving economically disadvantaged children the same chance to develop as their more fortunate peers, and addressing children's total needs by providing—where finances permit—an integrated package of services in health care, nutrition, and psychosocial stimulation.

Even a cursory consideration of these goals shows that commitment to a policy focused on the whole child may require countries to reassess their national priorities. But if there is enough political will to do so, the potential gains are great. More than thirty years of experimenting with early intervention programs have shown that there is no quick way to optimize the growth and development of a child. Supportive parenting, comprehensive health care (including clean water and sanitation), developmentally appropriate schooling, and good child care practices must persist throughout childhood, and program needs must be tailored to community requirements and budgets. What is clear is that we need to reassess the economics of early child development programs. We need to review the roles of NGOs, government, and the private sector. And we need to identify alternative sources of financing to fund early child development programs.

Approaches to the Development of Young Children

You can always spot Comprehensive Preschool Education Program children. They are more enthusiastic about taking part in activities, and they know much more than the others.

– Nese Postalcilar, Istanbul nursery school teacher

Whether preschool programs focus on improving parents' teaching and child care skills, delivering services directly to the children, or improving the child care services available in the community, their ultimate goal is to improve young children's capacity to develop and learn. The most effective programs combine basic nutrition and health care services with activities designed to stimulate the children's mental, language, physical, and psychosocial skills—all of which are mutually reinforcing. Experience and research have definitively shown that enhancing the experience of children—particularly disadvantaged children—from their youngest years substantially improves their potential for growth and development throughout life.

Program Design Options

Young children develop in the home, in day care centers, and in the community. But whether home-based or center-based, all preschool programs can consist of a combination of the following complementary approaches:

- *Delivering services to children.* Although usually center-based, this approach can also be used in the home. Its goal is to attend to the immediate needs of children. Examples include the U.S. Head Start program, Bolivia's Integrated Child Development Project, Colombia's Community Child Care and Nutrition Project, and India's Integrated Child Development Project.
- *Training caregivers and educating parents.* This approach seeks to show parents and caregivers how to improve their interaction with young children and how to improve the quality of care these children receive, enriching their environment and thereby enhancing their development. Examples include Mexico's Initial Education Project and Chile's Parent and Children Program.
- *Promoting community development and helping women to achieve development objectives.* This strategy stresses community initiative,

Table 1 Complementary program approaches for early child development

Program approach	*Participants and beneficiaries*	*Objectives*	*Models and examples*
Delivering services	■ Children aged 0–2 and 3–6 years	**Child** ■ Survival ■ Overall development ■ Socialization ■ Caregiver child care	■ Home day care (Colombia, Bolivia) ■ Integrated child development centers (India, Brazil) ■ "Add-on" centers (Ghana, Senegal) ■ Preschools, formal and nonformal (Peru)
Educating caregivers	■ Parents, family ■ Siblings	**Caregiver (mother)** ■ Create awareness ■ Change attitudes ■ Improve or change practices	■ Home visiting (Indonesia, Peru) ■ Parental education (China) ■ Child-to-child programs (Jamaica, Chile)
Promoting community involvement	■ Promoters ■ Leaders	**Community** ■ Increase awareness ■ Mobilize for action ■ Change conditions	■ Technical mobilization (Malaysia) ■ Social mobilization (Thailand)
Strengthening national resources and capabilities	■ Program personnel—professionals and paraprofessionals	**Caregivers (staff)** ■ Create awareness ■ Improve skills ■ Increase teaching materials	■ Training (Kenya) ■ Experimental demonstration projects ■ Strengthening infrastructure (Nigeria)

Table 1 continues on the next page

organization, and participation to create a basis for the political and social changes needed to correct conditions adversely affecting child development. It usually requires extensive involvement and assistance from nongovernmental organizations engaged in the community and considerable sensitivity to local cultural needs. By providing safe and affordable child care, these programs allow mothers the opportunity to pursue work

Table 1 (continued)

Program approach	*Participants and beneficiaries*	*Objectives*	*Models and examples*
Strengthening public awareness and stimulating demand	■ Policymakers ■ Public ■ Education professionals	**Public and government** ■ Create awareness ■ Build political will ■ Increase demand ■ Change attitudes	■ Social marketing (Jamaica) ■ Disseminating information (Nigeria)
Developing supportive legal frameworks	■ Working women with young children ■ Working children	**Public and government** ■ Increase awareness of rights and legal resources ■ Increase adoption of legislation recommended by the International Labour Organisation ■ Increase monitoring of and compliance with international human rights conventions	■ Workplace day care facilities (Brazil) ■ Protective environmental standards (India) ■ Maternal leave and benefits (Colombia) ■ Supporting breastfeeding for working mothers
Developing national child care and family policies	■ Families with young children	**Government, employers** ■ Encourage family-sensitive employment practices	■ Innovative public-private arrangements (India, Colombia) ■ Tax incentives for formal and quasiformal private enterprises

Source: Adapted from Consultative Group on Early Childhood Care and Development 1992, p. 22.

outside the home. Some mothers earn income by establishing child care facilities for community children in their homes. Examples include the Colombia Community Child Care and Nutrition and Promesa projects and the Bolivia Integrated Child Development Project.

■ *Strengthening institutional resources and capacity.* This approach seeks to strengthen the institutions responsible for implementing early child interventions. Examples include Kenya's early education centers, and World Bank–supported projects in Bolivia, Mexico, and Nigeria that have as a secondary objective strengthening institutional capacity for early child development interventions.

■ *Building public awareness and strengthening demand.* This approach focuses on producing and disseminating the information needed to create awareness of—and demand for—early childhood services. It targets parents, community leaders, and policymakers—as in Nigeria's Development Communications Project.

Phasing the Introduction of Inputs

Because human development is a dynamic process that unfolds in a predictable sequence—notwithstanding variations from individual to individual and culture to culture—it is possible to tailor early child development activities to developmental stages that roughly correspond to age groups. The need to ensure health and safety, however, cuts across all ages and is fundamental to future success. Clearly, a malnourished child or one debilitated by diarrheal disease cannot learn. But since much has been written on the subject of health and nutrition (see, for instance, the World Bank's *World Development Report 1993: Investing in Health*), the following description of essential inputs focuses on those related to mental stimulation and learning. Table 2 summarizes inputs deemed necessary to meet children's basic needs at each of the early developmental stages.

Table 2 What children need at different stages of development

Age (years)	*Basic needs*	*Inputs*
Birth to 1	Protection from physical danger Adequate nutrition Adequate health care Attachment to an adult Motor and sensory stimulation Appropriate language stimulation	Safe shelter Food and micronutrients Basic health care (immunization, oral rehydration therapy, hygiene) Age-appropriate developmental curriculum Supportive parents
1 to 3	All of the above, plus support in: Acquiring motor, language, and thinking skills Developing independence Learning self-control Play (to achieve all of the above)	Safe shelter Food and micronutrients Basic health care (all of the above, plus deworming) Age-appropriate developmental curriculum Supportive parents
3 to 6	All of the above, plus the opportunity to: Develop fine motor skills by manipulating the environment Expand language skills by talking, reading, and singing Learn cooperation by helping and sharing Experiment with prewriting and prereading skills	Safe shelter Food and micronutrients Basic health care (including deworming) Age-appropriate developmental curriculum Supportive parents
6 to 8	All of the above, plus the opportunity to: Develop numeracy skills Develop reading skills Engage in problem-solving activities Practice teamwork Develop sense of personal competency and self-worth Develop questioning and observation skills Acquire basic life skills	Safe shelter Food and micronutrients Basic health care (including deworming) Psychosocial development Basic education Age-appropriate developmental curriculum Supportive parents

Source: Based on Donohue-Colletta 1992 and information provided by Judith L. Evans of the Consultative Group on Early Childhood Care and Development.

In devising a teaching method tailored to the needs of very young learners, education researchers have relied on two basic observations: that children learn best from their own experience, and that their learning needs change as they progress through different stages of development. Active learning is a teaching method based on these two insights. An alternative to the traditional "skill and drill" method, active learning is far better suited to the needs of very young children (box 4).

Briefly outlined, active learning uses the following methods to achieve goals appropriate to each developmental stage:

- *Infants (birth to age one).* In active learning programs the focus for infants is on interaction with caregivers, who talk to the children, engage actively in their feeding, and frequently touch them, respond to them, and show affection. The caregivers' role is to provide an environment that is safe for infants to explore actively, one with a wide variety of objects that children can safely see, hear, smell, and taste during play.
- *Toddlers (age one to three).* For toddlers active learning means having the opportunity to explore an environment safely yet actively and to play with a variety of objects and games. Play objects need not be manufactured toys or purchased equipment but can be items such as pots, pans, cooking utensils, and containers that children can use in a variety of ways to learn about physical relationships and problem solving (box 5). Toddlers need to continue to interact with adults, and they need to interact with other children, which teaches them the social skills of cooperation, helping, and sharing. To develop children's mental skills, adults frequently read to them and engage them in conversation. To develop their gross motor skills, children will need a safe place in which to run, jump, climb, play with balls, and otherwise play actively.
- *Preschoolers (age three to six).* Active learning for preschoolers entails engaging in simple problem-solving tasks; developing such self-care

Box 4 An active learning approach

The High/Scope curriculum approach is an active learning method appropriate for children and validated by years of research (Hohmann and Weikart 1995). High/Scope researchers have found that—given time and opportunity—children aged two and a half to five years will:

- *Act out of their own interests and intentions.* Children engaged in active learning talk eagerly about their intentions. And because their motivation is internal, they become focused in their actions and thoughts. Given time and basic materials, children can generally muster, on their own or with a little adult help, whatever they need to fulfill their plans (a smock, a green block, a friend).
- *Choose materials and decide what to do with them.* Encouraging children to make choices both allows them to experiment and builds their confidence in their decisions. Active learning techniques thus involve introducing choice into all activities, including such tasks as zipping up coats and washing hands. Real choice is deciding not just what to do but how to do it.
- *Explore materials with all their senses and discover relationships through direct experience with objects, including transforming and combining materials.* Children actively seeking to satisfy their curiosity about materials that are new to them squeeze, drop, taste, smell, take apart, and climb on or under them to learn what they are, how they fit together, and how they work.
- *Use tools appropriate to their age.* Three-year-olds who can coordinate two or more actions can use equipment ranging from wheeled toys and swings to cameras, eggbeaters, and staplers. Using these items helps develop coordination, range of motion, and motor skills, which in turn enables children to do more on their own and to solve more complex problems.
- *Learn with their whole bodies.* Eager to stretch their physical abilities, young children climb on top of blocks, roll on the floor, twirl until they are dizzy, move chairs, and try to lift their friends. Active learning sites must be big enough for children to exercise their large muscles, and must contain lots of items that can be safely pushed, thrown, lifted, kicked, and carried.
- *Talk about their experiences.* Talking, besides developing language and social skills, builds children's confidence in the effectiveness of their own way of speaking. The active learning approach encourages children to talk over what they want to do with adults, to set their own agenda, to talk about an activity as it proceeds, to talk about what they have done, and to talk about any other meaningful experiences. Encouraging children to speak out gives them the confidence to define what they think and to revise their observations as their knowledge and abilities develop. The goal is to have children talk about what they see and think as a natural part of their lives.

Box 4 continues on the next page

skills as dressing and eating; developing the social skills needed to interact with adults and other children; and developing such cognitive skills as telling stories, associating the written word with spoken language, drawing pictures on their own about their play, and listening and moving to music.

Box 4, continued

Adults in High/Scope preschool programs set the stage for children to learn. Their job is to organize environments and routines, establish a climate for positive social interaction, and encourage students' expressed interests, problem-solving activities, and verbal reflections. To do this job, teachers, parents, and other caregivers need to:

- *Provide a variety of age-appropriate materials.* The greater the variety, the greater the children's scope to choose, manipulate, and combine materials, and thus to learn from the physical world.
- *Organize the space and allow time for children to use the materials.* Adults in the High/Scope Program divide the learning area into zones, each well stocked with objects organized around a theme (such as art, blocks, toys, or sand and water). The day is divided into periods for plan-work-recall, small-group, large-group, and outside activities. The largest block of time is devoted to plan-work-recall activities in which children choose and work with materials throughout the center. In small-group activities an adult chooses the area and materials and lets six to eight children work together. In large-group activities all of the children sing songs, do movement exercises, or otherwise perform as a group. Children can use outside time to play with wheeled toys, materials from nature, and swings and other outside equipment. The adults provide the framework needed for individual learning, continually observing, listening, and encouraging children's initiatives throughout the day.
- *Seek out children's intentions.* Encouraging children's intentions is a basic tenet of active learning. To discern a child's intentions, adults can ask directly or learn by observing. To show that they value the children's opinions, caregivers in the High/Scope Program affirm the children in their choices and actions.
- *Listen to children and encourage them to think.* Children learn best when they reflect on their actions. High/Scope caregivers make frequent comments that repeat, amplify, or build on what a child says. The caregivers frequently pause in their conversations with children to give the children time to think and speak. Encouraging children to speak strengthens their emerging ability to reason.
- *Encourage children to do things for themselves.* Because children learn more when they solve problems for themselves, High/Scope adults are taught to be understanding of mishaps and patient while children perform such everyday tasks as putting away toys or wiping up a spill (a common task in active learning classrooms). Adults can also help by referring children to other children for ideas, assistance, and conversation. Children should be encouraged to ask questions and to try to answer their questions themselves.

- *Young school-age children (age six to eight).* Young school-age children are interested in real-life tasks and activities, pretending and fantasy, and rules and rituals. Active learning encourages them to do all of these things and to explore their interests with friends. Through these activities they build a sense of teamwork and learn the importance of following

Box 5 Buy tools, not toys

That's what UNICEF is counseling preschool learning programs to do these days. For while everyone likes the idea of bright blocks and Legos, purchasing imported toys can break a preschool program's budget.

In past years donors often stocked the programs they sponsored with imported toys. But according to UNICEF experts, everything young children need to help them learn and grow can be found in parents' kitchens, cupboards, and backyards, and cheap, locally produced toys can usually replace expensive imports. By supplying communities with tools—from nails and paint to sewing machines—UNICEF is helping them to make the playthings their preschoolers need, support local entrepreneurs, hone local artisans' skills, and save preschool programs' precious resources.

What the curious toddler needs

Young children need materials that can be explored safely with all the senses—items they can hold, climb on, toss, throw, taste, drop, take apart, and put back together. They can learn as much from the inexpensive, everyday objects around them as from commercial toys.

Objects from the natural environment. These might include acorns, nuts, leaves, shells, pinecones, sand, and stones. Games children can play with these objects include sorting, counting, making designs, and stacking.

Found objects. Taken from the local environment, these objects can be used as they are or combined to make new playthings. They might include:

- Bottle caps, for sorting, stacking, counting, and making designs.
- Plastic bottles, to be filled and made into shakers or cut and used for pouring water or sand.
- Scraps of material, to make dolls, beanbags, and toss toys.
- Empty food boxes, to make stacking blocks.
- Tin cans, to be painted for sorting by size and color.
- Old clothes, to be used for dress-up or cut apart for scrap material.
- Toilet paper tubes, to be cut in different lengths, painted, sorted, and used for artwork.
- Thread spools, to be counted, sorted, and used to make designs.
- Heavy cardboard, to be cut and used as threading boards and puzzles.
- Corncobs, to be shellacked, painted, and cut to different lengths for sorting and making designs.

Messy materials. Children love—and learn a great deal from—playing with such messy materials as clay, paints, paste, sand, dough, and soap and water.

Tools and other objects adults use. These might include mops, brooms, buckets, screwdrivers, small (clawless) hammers, cooking utensils, and round-ended scissors.

Source: Derived from information supplied by Judith L. Evans, Consultative Group on Early Childhood Care and Development, August 1995.

rules. Active learning also helps children gain a sense of accomplishment, through cooking, making crafts, and working with such materials as wood and clay.

Designing a Program

Given the right opportunities and the right learning environment, children will develop in similar ways whatever their background. . . . As long as we keep in mind that everything we do is concerned with the development of the whole child, we are all doing the same sorts of things for the same sorts of reasons.

– Dr. Stephen Ngaruiya (as quoted in Bernard van Leer Foundation 1994, p. 9)

Countries everywhere find it difficult to implement programs for preschool-age children on a large scale. Experience has shown the importance of first fitting program approaches to societal needs and sociocultural characteristics and then defining clearly, from the outset, the processes for targeting the children most in need, training staff, and monitoring and evaluating programs.

Targeting. To achieve maximum results with limited funds, interventions must be targeted to reach only those children most in need and most likely to benefit. Proper targeting is an essential part of any social service program. If, for instance, a country has a severe problem with infant malnutrition, it would be inefficient to provide food supplements to all children under the age of fifteen. But by narrowing eligibility on the basis of age group and nutritional status, the program would be able to reach more of those most in need.

Thus one of a preschool program's first tasks is to establish the criteria for eligibility. The North American experience indicates that the poorest children benefit most—in both psychosocial and educational terms—from early child development programs (Campbell and Ramey 1994; Schweinhart 1992). Early child development programs should therefore be designed to reach the largest possible number of children living in poverty or in communities marked by a high prevalence of malnutrition, for these are the children who risk having their mental, social, and emotional development delayed or even permanently stunted.

Programs seeking to achieve different objectives also need to target by age as well as by income. Programs in the United States (WIC, Head Start), the former Soviet states, and India target very young children as the group most vulnerable and most likely to benefit from an intervention program. Children aged three to six, for instance, may need activities to prepare them for school, while for those under the age of two, proper nutrition, health care, and psychosocial stimulation are more critical. The U.S. eight-site Infant Health and Development Program, which targeted low-birth-weight and premature infants, demonstrated how early intervention could enhance these infants' cognitive, behavioral, and physical development.

Programs may also need to define eligibility criteria for services offered to mothers. India, for instance, considers women who are pregnant, lactating, or between the ages of fifteen and forty-five eligible for Integrated Child Development Services (ICDS).

Finally, countries can limit services geographically to make sure that they meet the needs of particular populations or settlement groups. India, for instance, targets areas inhabited predominantly by disadvantaged tribes and scheduled castes (India, Department of Women and Children 1988). Colombia has extended its urban slum programs to reach low-income rural areas as well. And Mauritius's Export Processing Zone (EPZ) Labor Welfare Fund, which covers only the families of EPZ workers, locates its child care centers within or near EPZ industrial estates (table 3).

While limiting eligibility for particularly expensive services is another way to limit costs, targeting is not always easy. India, for instance, has attempted to restrict its expensive supplementary food services to mothers and children who are demonstrably malnourished. But almost half of ICDS supervisors reported that food services were delivered to women and children who did not qualify for them (NIPCCD 1992).

Involving parents and communities. Colombia and India have both noted that rates of use of early child development programs are low

Table 3 Targeting characteristics in four countries

Country and program	*Age of children*	*Mother targeted*	*Targeted community*	*Screening criteria*
Colombia (Hogares Comunitarios de Bienestar)	2 to 6 years	Yes	Self-targeting of low-income urban areas	None
India (Integrated Child Development Services)	0 to 6 years	Yes	Low-income groups, disadvantaged tribes, scheduled castes	Feeding program meant to be restricted
Kenya (Early Child Education)	3 to 6 years	No	Self-targeting	None
Mauritius (EPZ Labor Welfare Fund)	3 months to 3 years	No	Export processing zones	Priority given to children of EPZ employees

Source: Wilson 1995.

among eligible populations—in large part, according to a recent evaluation study in India, because the target population was unaware that such services were offered. In addition, working mothers in India found it inconvenient to attend two- or three-hour sessions during the day. And even Colombia's day-long child care was not sufficient where parents worked more than eight hours a day. To be useful to families, therefore, day care programs must be both well advertised and tailored to meet local needs.

Many countries claim to have tried to involve community groups and parents in program development and delivery. But despite the putative emphasis on local involvement, community participation in India's ICDS program, for instance, remains marginal. Even after fifteen years of program operation, most of the community representatives questioned had never been consulted during the initial stages of a preschool education project, and many were unaware that their participation was needed.

One way to involve community members is to use volunteer caregivers. But relying on volunteers can be problematic because it sends the message that preschool programs are of little importance and that caregiving is not a viable career. As a result, many volunteers are dissatisfied and seek to be recognized as government workers, and the turnover rate is high. In Colombia, for instance, where the government pays each home day care mother a small stipend for each child in her care and parents pay an additional fee, home day care workers' earnings are capped at 65 percent of the average national income plus social security contributions and access to home improvement loans. Although such loans are granted for up to five years, home day care mothers generally stay in the Colombian program only two years.

Indian caregivers and their helpers receive honorariums set at 75 percent of the national per capita income. The Indian caregivers' union, created in the 1980s, has been pressuring the government to admit them into the civil service. In response, India now proposes to consider preschool caregivers with secondary education and ten years of experience for government appointments as supervisors and project officers.

Defining a curriculum. Some experts on early child development have suggested that, provided a child receives proper care and has interesting activities and other children to play with, the actual type of preschool experiences matters very little (Osborn and Milbank 1987). Increasingly, however, experts favor approaches that are more educational, maintaining that failure to adopt a specific viewpoint or curriculum model leads to poor-quality education.

Early child development programs need to have a curriculum that is well defined—one that is designed to promote children's development and based on validated models, and that emphasizes children's choice, decisionmaking, and active learning. As illustrated in table 4, approaches are likely to differ on the basis of people's beliefs about how

Table 4 Three approaches to the education of young children based on three different theories of learning

Educational approach	*Child's role*		*Teacher's role*	
	Active	*Passive*	*Active*	*Passive*
Cognitive development[a]	X		X	
Play-based nursery school[b]	X			X
Didactic[c]		X	X	
Custodial care[d]		X		X

a. Based on Jean Piaget's constructivist theory.
b. Traditional center-based method, based on the British Infant School movement.
c. Uses behaviorist model of didactic instruction reinforced by systematic awards.
d. Not considered an educational approach.
Source: Based on Roopnarine and Johnson 1993.

children learn and the role of the teacher. Teachers and caregivers need to understand the curriculum selected and be trained to make decisions about what to do in the classroom based on their understanding of the curriculum's theoretical base. They will therefore need ongoing training and supervision from someone trained in that educational technique. The underlying theory will govern staff training and the methods used to deliver the service.

Structured programs have the added advantage that they can be evaluated on the basis of existing standards for interaction and activities for young children, and methods proved to be successful in the field can be widely applied. By contrast, unstructured collections of ideas—even good ideas—cannot be evaluated or replicated, and the quality of the outcomes cannot, therefore, be maintained. Adopting a specific, valid, theoretical approach is therefore the first step toward instituting an effective early child development program.

While it is not yet possible to rate the effectiveness of different approaches on the basis of evidence from developing countries, data from the United States and England suggest that which active learning curriculum is chosen is less important than whether active learning techniques are used consistently and well.

The following guidelines are offered for the implementation of any early child development program:

- Design a program that meets children's educational and psychosocial needs as well as their physical needs. Children most need a supportive environment in which they are free to choose their own learning activities, to take responsibility for completing them, and to talk about what they have accomplished.
- Train in-service staff to carry out this program.
- Provide supportive supervision.

- Keep groups to no more than sixteen to twenty three- to five-year-olds for every two adults, twelve two-year-olds for every two adults, or eight one-year-olds for every two adults. Most important is not necessarily the size of the group of children but that there are two adults.
- Emphasize the need for staff to be sensitive to children's physical, health, and nutrition needs and their families' child care and social service needs.
- Evaluate procedures for their appropriateness to different stages of the children's development.

Low-income developing countries that wish to begin focusing on hygiene, nourishment, health, and mental stimulation could set up integrated early child development programs that:

- Provide children with a secure space for movement and play.
- Provide flexible multifunctional furniture that can be handled by children.
- Provide adequate food and clean water for drinking and washing.
- Provide children with material especially adapted for handling, experimenting, and playing.

Selecting and training staff. The quality and consistency of child care staff have been identified as among the major determinants of a program's efficacy. The U.S. National Child Care Staffing Study (Childcare Employee Project 1992) documented that children in centers with rapid staff turnover spent less time engaged in social activities with peers and more time wandering about aimlessly, and showed disturbing lags in their social and language development. A study commissioned by the California General Assembly found that in classes in which the ratio of children to teachers was too high, children were less involved in classroom activities. Better outcomes for the children were significantly correlated with higher staff wages and benefits (Childcare Employee Project 1992).

Despite these findings, however, the fact remains that most preschool programs in developing countries rely heavily on volunteer caregivers. And because they are volunteers, the criteria for their selection have been relatively flexible. In India, for instance, caregivers are expected to be literate, but illiteracy has been cited as a serious problem (NIPCCD 1992).

Colombia's home-based program requires only that caregivers be twenty to forty-five years of age, have no more than two young children, and own their homes—although women with writing, reading, and basic mathematical skills are preferred. Those interested in becoming caregivers must attend a forty-hour workshop offered by national child development representatives. The most promising candidates are then selected by the national representative in concert with the parents association managing the program locally. In Kenya preschool teachers are selected by parents and local authorities and are expected to receive six training sessions, totaling eighteen weeks, over a two-year period. Yet in 1993 less than 40 percent had completed their training. A major factor was lack of funding. In India, too, trained government program officers and supervisors have had difficulties passing along what they have learned to local providers. The reason they cite is that sites are inaccessible and too numerous for trainers to be able to maintain the schedule. In Mauritius, by contrast, where the preschool programs do not rely on volunteers, staff have at least a secondary education and are recruited locally.

To upgrade staff training and improve the quality of early childhood education programs, policymakers must therefore:

- Define and adopt effective training practices.
- Set up a system for training teachers throughout the country.
- Schedule preservice and in-service teacher training.
- Identify professional and paraprofessional caregivers who should receive training.
- Make training requirements flexible enough to suit a variety of early childhood program settings.
- Make training requirements flexible enough to be adaptable to the needs of different cultures.

Assessing children's progress. Because young children need different inputs at different stages of their intellectual and emotional development, preschool caregivers must screen their progress regularly. But this is no easy task.

Developmental measures for young children are notoriously unstable, and no single indicator can accurately capture a child's well-being or readiness to learn. School performance is affected by many factors other than cognitive ability—such as physical well-being, emotional security, social confidence, language fluency, learning disabilities, interests, engagement, approach to learning, the presence of a parent or guardian to explain things, and general knowledge and skills. The danger always exists that assessment tools will be used to exclude or track certain classes of children, making it undesirable to use standardized tests to signal readiness for school. The only defensible criterion for school entry is attainment of the legal chronological age.

But in early childhood development programs continual screening is a necessity. A recent review of instruments for assessing children's psychosocial development recommended that children be tested and regularly reevaluated for specific indicators, determined by each program's objectives (Landers and Kagitcibasi 1990). Working together, the Tufts University School of Nutrition in Boston and the Diponegoro University School of Medicine in Java devised a "cultural-specific inventory of child development milestones," derived from focus group discussions, concept testing, and formative evaluations (table 5). Now thoroughly tested and refined, the Tufts-Diponegoro chart is being used to study the progress of children under three as part of Indonesia's National Growth Monitoring Program (Landers and Kagitcibasi 1990).

Table 5 Child development chart used in Indonesia

Age (months)	*Developmental milestone*	*Stimulation message*
0	Inspects surroundings	Hold baby facing you, talk and smile. Play every day.
1	Smiles in response to person	Hold baby facing you, talk and smile. Play every day.
2	Holds head up	Place baby on stomach and talk to him or her.
3	Eyes follow dangling ring	Dangle item. Let baby watch it move.
4	Makes three different sounds	Talk to baby, explain what you're doing.
5	Picks up small item	Sit baby up, give him or her small items to reach for.
6	Looks for fallen object	Hide toys and help baby find them.
7	Sits alone steadily	Let baby sit up with a little help.
8	Plays peek-a-boo	Play peek-a-boo.
9	Picks up object with thumb and one finger	Give baby small items to pick up.
10	Responds to verbal request	Help baby to wave or clap.
11	Uncovers toy	Cover toy while baby is looking. Help him or her find it.
12	Walks alone	Let baby walk holding onto your hand.
13	Imitates adult	Show child how to do what you do.
14	Stacks two cubes	Give child small boxes or blocks of wood to stack.
15	Says two or more words	Encourage child to repeat names of objects or activities.
16	Brings object on request	Ask child to bring you things (two-part directions).
17	Points to three body parts	Teach child parts of the body.
18	Feeds self with spoon	Teach child to use spoon.
19	Speaks in two-word sentences	Expand one-word sentences into two-word sentences.
20	Points to three pictures	Point to pictures and name them for child.
21	Builds a tower of four cubes	Give the child small boxes or wood blocks to play with.
22	Discriminates between two objects	Tell child stories.
23	Kicks ball, balances on one foot	Show child how to kick a ball.
24	Names three objects	Have child repeat names of objects after you.

Source: Landers and Kagitcibasi 1990.

Assessing a program's success. Early child development researchers today can confidently assert that enriched early childhood experiences permanently enhance children's competence in everyday life—that is, their ability to meet social expectations, advance appropriately in school, stay out of trouble, and have high aspirations for themselves (Schweinhart and Weikart 1980). But contrary to earlier theories, this benefit—as the High/Scope Perry Preschool study has shown—does not derive from improved intellectual performance (Schweinhart, Barnes, and Weikart 1993). The success of an early child development program therefore cannot be measured by whether or not participants' IQ scores rise five or ten points.

Katz (1992) proposes that preschool programs be judged in large part by children's long-term satisfaction with them, as reflected in the degree to which they feel intellectually engaged and respected. High/Scope researchers, again in the High/Scope Perry Preschool study, further maintain that children from successful early childhood interventions experience greater success in their first weeks in school, which then increases their motivation and leads to better school performance and higher regard from teachers and classmates. More successful school careers in turn increase the chance that children will graduate from high school, hold jobs, and not turn to crime.

Since early child development programs ideally integrate a variety of services, assessment indicators are required in the areas of health, nutrition, psychosocial and cognitive development, and parental and community factors. Specific indicators relevant to each program's objectives must be identified at the outset so that mechanisms for monitoring and evaluation can be put in place (table 6).

Preschool programs in Bolivia, Indonesia, and Turkey, for instance, are being judged on such outcome variables for participating children as anthropometric data, immunization status, psychosocial development (Bolivia uses a specially adapted development scale), and schooling (age at entry, dropout and repetition rates, academic performance, behavior). Outcome variables for participating mothers include personal health, participation in the labor force, education level, knowledge of child-rearing practices, and self-confidence. A valuational instrument sensitive to the many and varied effects of early child development programs is badly needed, both to help standardize the evaluation of such programs and to make supervision of them more effective.

Most early child development projects have been able to do little more in the way of self-evaluation than to list the number of their participants and describe the extent and content of services offered. Impact evaluations tend to be limited. They are by nature difficult because the time lag between the intervention and the expected benefits is far longer than the duration of projects, often five to seven years.

Colombia's Hogares Comunitarios de Bienestar (Community Child Care and Nutrition Project, or HCB), for instance, certainly

Table 6 Indicators for assessing the success of early child development programs based on potential benefits

Beneficiary group	*Area of change*	*Indicators of change*
Children	Psychosocial development	Improved cognitive development (thinking, reasoning); improved social development (relationships to others); improved emotional development (self-image, security); improved language skills
	Health and nutrition	Increased survival chances; reduced morbidity; improved hygiene; improved weight and height for age; improved micronutrient balances
	Progress and performance in primary school	Higher chance of entering; less chance of repeating; higher learning and better performance
Adults (program staff, parents) and siblings	General health knowledge, general health attitudes and practices	Improved health and hygiene; improved nutrition (own status); preventive medical monitoring and attention; timely treatment; improved diet
	Self-esteem Relationships Employment	Improved relationships between husband and wife, between parents and older children; caregivers freed to seek or improve employment; new employment opportunities created by program; increased market for program-related goods
Communities	Physical environment Social participation Solidarity	Improved sanitation; more spaces for play; new facilities; greater female participation; greater demand for existing services; community projects benefiting all
Schools and health service facilities	Efficiency	Better attention to health; changed user practices; reduced school repetition and dropout
	Effectiveness Capacity Practice and content	Greater coverage; improved ability, confidence, or organization; methods and curriculum content
Society	Health and education status Participation Productivity Delinquency Fertility Equality	Fewer days lost to sickness; a healthier population; a more literate, educated population; greater social participation; a more productive labor force; reduced delinquency; reduced fertility; reduced social inequality

Source: Myers 1995.

Box 6 Indicators used in Bolivia

Bolivia's Integrated Child Development Project—supported by the World Bank, U.S. Agency for International Development (USAID), and public and private donors—targets poor households in urban areas of more than 10,000 inhabitants. The project proposes to install 9,000 day care centers between 1993 and 1999. Every year these centers will provide informal, home-based, integrated child development services to more than 200,000 children aged six months to six years—roughly 16 percent of all Bolivian children living in urban areas. An estimated 16,000 pregnant women will also benefit directly from the project, either as caregivers or as the mothers of children in project day care centers.

To improve information on Bolivia's young children, the project will conduct an integrated household survey, which will allow it to compare outcomes for participants and nonparticipants. The project's management information system will include detailed information on day care administration and financing, the number of day care centers available, the number of caregivers and of children enrolled, the duration of children's attendance, and children's health and developmental status (as defined by the presence of health cards, nutritional status, vaccinations, number of health visits, weight, and other developmental indicators).

helped many children (UNICEF 1993). But attempts to assess the project's impact more precisely were skewed because they compared groups of children from the same project (that is, those who had attended the program for three months or less with those who had attended nine months or more), underestimating the fact that the groups would reflect the same selection bias. Yet the evaluation has proved useful in further improving program implementation. Children who had attended for a year, it was found, still suffered nutritional deficiencies at a rate above the national average—suggesting a need to improve community food purchasing and delivery systems. A later census confirmed that fully a fifth of HCB homes had no program food supplements on hand and that nearly a third had not received the complete nutritional benefits offered under the program.

By contrast, Bolivia's Integrated Child Development Project started off with a project impact evaluation scheme in place (box 6). From the outset to the end of the project, data are being gleaned from household surveys of both participants and nonparticipants. Evaluators will use this information to assess the project's success at targeting high-risk children, women, and families; its effect on the development and well-being of both participants and communities; and its effect on children's later performance in school.

It is somewhat easier to evaluate early childhood interventions whose major thrust is improving the diet and health of mothers and children (see description of WIC program in part II). India's massive

Integrated Child Development Services, for instance, has been evaluated frequently over the years. A recent review of nearly thirty nutrition impact studies confirmed that the ICDS program—even operating at a minimal level of quality—has had a positive impact on children under six. A 1984–86 comparative study found higher infant mortality rates in

Box 7 India's first Tamil Nadu Integrated Nutrition Project

Twenty years ago 85 percent of children under six in Tamil Nadu were underweight, and malnutrition contributed to three-quarters of all infant and toddler deaths. India's first Tamil Nadu Integrated Nutrition Project (TINP I) was designed to reach the populations most at risk—weaning children, pregnant and nursing mothers, and adolescent girls. One of the largest nutrition projects in the world, it reached more than 13 million people from 1980 to 1989. Its US$81 million cost was funded in part by a US$32 million International Development Association–approved loan in 1980.

The project's goals were to halve the protein-energy malnutrition rate (roughly 60 percent for mothers and children in the state's worst-hit rural areas), to reduce by a quarter the infant mortality rate (then at about 125 per thousand), to reduce the rate of vitamin A deficiency in children under five from about 27 percent to 5 percent, and to lower the rate of nutritional anemia in pregnant and nursing women from about 55 percent to 20 percent.

Program design

The project provided a package of services in nutrition education, primary health care, immunization, and supplementary on-site feeding for severely malnourished children. In an innovative move, the project offered low-weight infants and toddlers—identified through monthly weighing—supplementary food for short periods to help them recover their growth, rather than offering prolonged feeding programs for older children. Closely supervised women, locally recruited and trained, delivered education and other services to 1,500 people at each of the project's 9,000 community nutrition centers. TINP I's high supervisor-to-worker ratio and intensive on-the-job training proved critical to its success.

What worked, what didn't

Identifying inappropriate child care practices as the root cause of most malnutrition, the project sought to change these practices through education. Problem cases were identified through monthly weighings, where mothers and nutrition workers could also meet to discuss concerns and exchange information. World Bank evaluators found that frequency of weighing, lower age at enrollment, and immunization were all significantly associated with improved nutritional status, while deworming and vitamin A supplements were not. TINP I recurrent costs have been estimated at US$9.41 per beneficiary for 1984–85, of which about 47 percent went for nutrition (30 percent for food) and 43 percent for health care (Berg 1987).

Box 7 continues on the next page

Box 7, continued

Under TINP I, weight-for-age improved steadily in Tamil Nadu, and malnutrition rates dropped for all ages served by the program. Children aged six months to three years gained more than 6 percent in weight, and these improvements lasted. Half to three-quarters of these gains are credited to TINP. Monitoring indicators suggest that the procedures for beginning and ending supplementary feeding, providing educational inputs, encouraging community participation, and keeping accurate records were carefully followed and that leakage to nonparticipants was small. Since scheduled-caste children's participation increased from 37 percent to 42 percent and the average age at enrollment declined, it also appears that the program became progressively more successful at reaching the neediest.

Lessons learned

TINP I has shown that education can change unhealthy child-rearing practices and that narrowly focused targeting is cost-effective. The project's success rested on:

- The careful selection of community nutrition workers.
- Detailed but simple work routines that emphasized outreach.
- Training to develop skills.
- Intensive and supportive supervision.
- Efforts to gain community support and generate enthusiasm for the project.

Source: World Bank 1995.

non-ICDS areas, and a study on the effects of primary education found that ICDS participants had higher primary school enrollment rates and better attendance and performance records. Among children from low and middle castes, primary school dropout rates were significantly lower for those served by ICDS (Consultative Group on Early Childhood Care and Development 1993). Another extensively evaluated program is the Tamil Nadu Integrated Nutrition Project (box 7).

Working with NGOs and Other Agencies

In many countries where both funding and infrastructure are too weak to support the provision of basic social services, private organizations—both local and international—step in to take up the slack. These non-governmental organizations frequently establish the administrative network needed to bring essential services to the poor, and in supplying these services, develop close ties with local people. NGOs have been particularly effective at mobilizing community support, training care-givers, and monitoring projects' progress when working with early child development interventions that target the poor.

Box 8 Aga Khan Foundation brings active learning into the madrasa

Because all societies value their children highly, programs aimed at the very young must be particularly sensitive to the local context. In East Africa, as in other areas where there are Muslim communities, young children receive religious education beginning in the preschool years in madrasas, or koranic schools. But with formal primary education increasingly influencing later economic opportunities, parents are seeking ways to ensure that their children gain the knowledge they need to succeed in the broader society as well as in their own cultural and religious environment. For nearly a decade, the Aga Khan Foundation has worked with Muslim communities on the coast of Kenya to find an appropriate solution.

Community leaders approached the Aga Khan Foundation because they were concerned about their children's low enrollment and success in the primary schools. Through the foundation's support, a pilot program—and later, the Madrasa Resource Center established in Mombasa—developed an integrated madrasa preschool curriculum through close consultation with local religious educators, using the Kenyan Institute of Education's preschool guidelines as a basic framework. The curriculum incorporated child-centered activities that strengthened preschoolers' social, physical, and cognitive skills, promoted activity-based learning for both religious and secular subjects, and strongly encouraged the use of local stories, songs, and games. With support from the Madrasa Resource Center, communities have provided classrooms, organized preschool committees, and nominated local women for training at the center.

Box 8 continues on the next page

Box 8, continued

An extensive review of the integrated madrasa preschool program highlighted important requirements for its success: increasing poor communities' ability to pay for preschool programs, strengthening local school committees' planning and management skills, including more women on school committees, enhancing the skills and capacity of the Madrasa Resource Center staff, and improving the quality of primary school education to consolidate early gains.

These needs will be addressed as the program scales up in the three countries over the next five years (1996–2000). In particular, the use of endowments to local community preschools will be tested to see whether this is a feasible way to achieve long-term financial sustainability for community-based education. Attention will also go to improving the quality of the curriculum and strengthening the training and supervision of teachers in order to improve their skills and their knowledge about working with preschoolers.

Despite these remaining issues, the popularity of the integrated madrasa preschools suggests that programs tailored to and designed and implemented by the community will meet local needs and can gain wide acceptance.

Source: Derived from information supplied by Kathy Bartlett, Aga Khan Foundation, October 1995.

Save the Children is an international NGO that has worked with at-risk children and families since 1932 and is now active in forty countries and twenty U.S. states. In 1991 it initiated the program Strong Beginnings, which seeks funding from governments and donors for large-scale programs in community-based primary education, adult literacy and nonformal education (especially for women), and children's early development. These areas were chosen because they are interrelated (literate mothers, for instance, are more likely to take better care of their children); need relatively little investment to achieve great improvements; are the shared responsibility of government, public and private institutions, communities, and families; and confer their greatest benefit on the poor—particularly poor women and girls.

Save the Children's efforts are paying off. Stand-alone early childhood programs supported by Strong Beginnings are now operating in Bangladesh, Bolivia, Costa Rica, Croatia, Jordan, Nepal, the Philippines, Thailand, the United States (New York), and the West Bank

Box 9 UNESCO's early childhood activities

In line with the statement in the United Nations' 1990 World Declaration on Education for All that "learning begins at birth," UNESCO supports families and communities as the most influential educators of young children. Active in UN-supported and other international early childhood initiatives, UNESCO encourages governments to include such programs in their social and economic planning, offers technical assistance, and acts as a clearinghouse for information about child care and family education programs, organizations, and policies. In addition to strengthening regional early childhood cooperation centers in individual countries, UNESCO has created a graduate-level degree program in early child development, sponsored workshops for administrators, and inventoried developing countries' resources and potential for early child development.

The United Nations—working with UNICEF, the World Health Organization (WHO), major institutes, and NGOs—provides its member states with support for early child development and family education programs in the Middle East, the Pacific, Latin America, and Southeast Asia. It also publishes some of the latest research data available on early childhood topics.

Family education

UNESCO seeks to improve children's home environments by giving parents the knowledge and skills they need to raise their children well. Information programs are particularly important where center-based programs are not feasible. Over the past three years UNESCO has supported twenty different parental information projects focusing on the development and education of young children.

Box 9 continues on the next page

Box 9, continued

Young Child and the Family Environment (YCFE) Project
Established in 1989, this project coordinates UNESCO's efforts under the UN Convention on the Rights of the Child, along with research and other activities in early childhood care and family education. Set up in 1990, the YCFE International Database contains information on roughly 1,500 organizations involved in early child development in 146 countries. UNESCO has published this information in its *International Directory on the Young Child and the Family Environment* (1991) and *Directory of Early Childhood Care and Education Organizations in Sub-Saharan Africa* (1992). Directories covering the Arab states and Asia and the Pacific—as well as a world sourcebook—are in the works.

Documenting early childhood activities
In addition to the YCFE database and publications, UNESCO maintains the Early Childhood Care and Education (ECCE) Database, which has information on policies, legislation, institutions, publications, databases, and major activities having to do with child development. It covers 116 countries and has been running since 1993. Each country profile contains national policy, coverage and supervision of programs, major actors, issues, problems encountered, successful initiatives, staff training and qualifications, media-based efforts, and parental and community involvement. In addition, UNESCO provides information and financial support to selected professional journals and reviews—including the *Coordinators' Notebook* published by the interagency Consultative Group on Early Childhood Care and Development.

Source: Based on information provided by UNESCO YCFE Project, September 1995.

and Gaza, and early childhood components are being included in women's literacy, savings, and health group programs and in community health and nutrition interventions. These early childhood interventions take place in homes, factories, and community centers and use a wide range of activities designed to enhance disadvantaged children's cognitive, physical, social, and emotional development—putting them on an equal footing with their more prosperous peers when they enter school.

Working together, such influential international NGOs as the Aga Khan Foundation, Bernard van Leer Foundation, Save the Children, and Christian Children's Foundation and the United Nations agencies UNICEF and UNESCO have sponsored workshops on setting up and running child development programs in Africa, Latin America, and the Middle East. And along with other interested agencies, they are presently cosponsoring an International Child Development Training Initiative.

Kenya's government has been working with a number of NGOs—including the Bernard van Leer Foundation and the Aga Khan Foundation—in collaboration with such UN agencies as UNICEF, since 1963 in its effort to develop a national early child development program as part of its self-help, or *harambee*, policy (Bernard van Leer Foundation 1994, pp. 8–9). Together they have set up many community preschool facilities, and Kenya established a National Center for Early Childhood Education to improve preschool teacher training.

Kenya today boasts a network of district training centers to instruct preschool teachers on the importance of play and the manipulation of materials from the environment to young children's learning and development. Teachers also learn how to provide the children with suitable materials, how to identify and help children with special needs, and how to involve parents and communities in stimulating young children's development and growth.

As a result of these efforts, trainers, teachers, parents, and local communities in Kenya routinely cooperate in developing early childhood curriculums and teaching materials. Parents and communities collect stories, riddles, poems, and games, which the child care program then has edited, reproduced, and distributed to other communities. Such joint efforts enhance the quality of teaching materials available and increase community satisfaction with the program. In addition, district training centers hold workshops for primary school children to encourage them to make toys and learning materials they can use in playing with younger children—benefiting children of all ages—and child care centers provide health and nutrition services and information to families.

Paying for Child Development Programs

Although the cost of providing child care services to young children has been studied in industrial countries, there is as yet little information regarding the cost in developing countries. Nor is the value of the benefits that children, mothers, and communities receive relative to the cost of providing different child service inputs known. The task remains, therefore, to determine the optimal level of services very young children need and the best ways to finance them.

Determining the Cost

Expenses for early child development programs can be divided among the following needs:

■ *Site.* Center-based programs have been estimated in some studies to cost up to five times as much as preschool programs in private homes, even where minimal home improvement costs are reimbursed. Any home that can provide a safe space, minimum sanitation facilities, and a kitchen is sufficient.

According to a recent study of six developing countries (Wilson 1995), only in Mauritius did a majority of child care facilities meet government standards (that is, had adequate toilet facilities, met fire and safety regulations, and had adequate indoor and outdoor play areas). Across all six countries, standards were lowest where sites were used for multiple purposes. In Colombia 70 percent of all sites were found to lack at least one basic site requirement (electricity, flushable toilet, wood or concrete flooring, and a child care room of at least 20 square meters (ICBF 1994), and over half were judged "miserable" (lacking in at least two areas). The Colombian Institute for Family Welfare (ICBF) is therefore supporting the establishment of municipal centers that could accommodate several groups of community mothers and children. In India, although communities are supposed to supply an adequate site for a preschool center (either by building it new or by adapting an existing building), less than a quarter of preschools now operating have adequate sewage disposal facilities, and 39 percent are housed in semipermanent structures.

■ *Equipment (weight scales, toys, informal materials for play, audiovisual and musical equipment).* While equipment needs will vary from program

to program, considerable savings can be realized where parents learn how to adapt ordinary objects and to make educational toys from materials found in the children's natural environment.

- *Food supplies.* Food is the most costly input in an early child development program and can account for up to 40 percent of program costs. Food is often provided by the government through the ministry of agriculture or by international donors such as the World Food Programme. While costs can be cut by involving the community in food provision, ensuring timely delivery and a sustainable supply of food supplements is generally logistically difficult. Cooperative food operations therefore require close supervision.
- *Staff (training and salaries).* Care providers for very young children can be trained or untrained teachers or day care workers, mothers, or other women from the community. Some caregivers are paid salaries; some are considered volunteers and receive small honorariums. Volunteers, however, cannot be held to as high a standard as employees, and many—dissatisfied with their status—demand salaries.
- *Supervision.* Ongoing supervision is necessary to make a program effective. The cost of supervision needs to be included in operations.
- *Evaluation.* In addition to monitoring program implementation, each project needs to incorporate in its design an evaluation of program impact.

Governments can contain costs by targeting services narrowly so that they reach only the neediest. Some have instituted cost-sharing measures, paid "volunteer" caregivers honorariums rather than hiring them as regular staff with benefits and salaries, and encouraged home-based rather than center-based care. These measures have generally failed to lower costs as much as expected, however, and in some instances have compromised program quality.

Box 10 Cost, quality, and child care outcomes

According to a recent study, only one in seven U.S. centers provides child care of a quality that promotes healthy development and learning, and almost half of the infants and toddlers in the 401 child care facilities observed spent their days in rooms of less than minimal quality (Helburn, Culkin, and others 1995). As might be expected, moreover, states with less stringent standards had more child care centers and classrooms of low quality. Yet the same study found that better-quality services cost, on average, just 10 percent more than mediocre care. These findings suggest that modest investments—when combined with reasonable regulation—could significantly improve early child care interventions.

Most of the centers studied offered services far below professional standards. But the study confirmed earlier findings that centers paying higher wages attracted better-quality staff. Quality varied most in the areas of wages and teachers' level of education and specialized training. Parents were not a good judge of quality, tending to overestimate the quality of the programs their children were attending. The study found that quality child care is associated most strongly with high staff-to-child ratios, high staff wages, well-trained staff, and experienced administrators.

Source: Helburn, Culkin, and others 1995.

Financing the Program

Most governments finance early childhood interventions out of their general revenues. The amount of public revenues paid for child care services is indicative of the importance of these services to the state—just as the share of private payments reflects their importance to families.

Families in industrial countries apparently put a high premium on child care services, which are estimated to cost a fourth to a half of the mother's salary. Although the relative share of public and private contributions varied in Belgium, Denmark, Italy, and Japan, Psacharopoulos (1982) found that in all these countries, both have increased slowly over time.

Public and shared funding. Many developing countries subsidize enriched child care services heavily to make sure that they are available to poor families, who already spend almost all of their income on food, housing, and transportation. Colombia's government, for instance, finances 85 percent of the costs of its Hogares Comunitarios de Bienestar program, primarily through a payroll tax set at 2 percent in 1974 and raised to 3 percent in 1988.

Most national governments share the cost of early childhood interventions with subnational governments and program beneficiaries (table 7). Kenya's central government, for instance, funds the training of caregivers, while local authorities provide and maintain preschool

Table 7 Cost-sharing arrangements in four countries

Country and program	*National government responsibilities*	*Subnational government responsibilities*	*Parents' responsibilities*
Colombia (Hogares Comunitarios de Bienestar)	Finances most HCB activities.	State and local governments do not contribute significantly.	Pay half of caregivers' honorariums and social security contributions. Do volunteer work.
India (Integrated Child Development Services)	Finances most ICDS activities except food program.	State government administers delivery of the ICDS program and finances the supplementary feeding program.	Do not contribute significantly.
Kenya (Early Child Education)	Finances training for caregivers.	Local government provides and maintains center sites.	Pay caregivers' honorariums.
Mauritius (EPZ Labor Welfare Fund)	Contributes about 10 percent of tripartite fund budget.	State and local governments do not contribute significantly.	Pay preschool fees (EPZ workers' fees are lower than those for non-EPZ workers).

Source: Wilson 1995.

program sites. India's national government pays for everything but supplementary feeding, which is financed by the states. In a bold and unusual move, the governor of Santa Catarina in Brazil assumed full responsibility for child-centered programs and combined the contributions he had elicited from each state government department to establish an intersectoral children's aid budget (Myers 1995).

Parents generally pay for caregivers' salaries. Colombian parents pay half of the caregivers' honorariums and social security contributions. Colombia's government, however, also finances a loan scheme to help mothers running *hogares comunitarios* (nurseries) to improve their homes. Until recently, parent associations were held responsible for defaults on these loans, but in the face of high default rates, the government has introduced a policy that makes the community mothers who run preschool programs liable for repayment if they leave the program.

User fees. A number of countries have instituted user fees to finance at least part of their early childhood interventions. Parents participating

Table 8 Four countries' early child development programs

Country, program, and objectives	*Beneficiaries and service sites*	*Service*	*Cost per child per year (US$)*[a]
India: Integrated Child Development Services (ICDS) Maternal and child health and nutrition Preschool education	2 million pregnant and lactating women 11.2 million children aged 0 to 6 205,000 sites, 1975–94	■ Provides pregnant and lactating women with 300 calories, 8 to 10 grams protein, iron and vitamin A supplements, and pre- and postnatal care. ■ Measures children's weight, height, and nutritional status monthly. ■ Provides medical referrals, immunization, diarrhea treatment, and deworming. ■ Offers 2 to 3 hours of preschool education.	$100
Colombia: Hogares Comunitarios de Bienestar Child health and nutrition, and preschool education	55,000 sites, 1987–94	■ Regularly measures weight, height, and nutritional status of children aged 2 to 6. ■ Provides one meal, two snacks daily (50 to 60 percent of average daily caloric needs). ■ Produces and distributes nutritional supplement *Bienestarina*. ■ Supports purchase of local fresh food. ■ Preschool education sessions during full-day care.	$140
Peru: Peru Non-formal Program of Initial Education (Pronoei) Preschool education	60,000 children aged 3 to 5	■ Provides food and physical, mental, and social development activities. ■ Teaches groups of 25 to 30 children several hours a day, four or five mornings most weeks of the year. ■ Trains paraprofessionals who run 10- to 14-day courses for mothers and periodic refresher sessions.	$40[b] ($28)[c]
Chile: Parents and Children Project (PPH) Early child development education for parents	Serves 200 communities	■ Produces 12 radio programs on the development of children aged 4 to 6. ■ Gathers families together once a week to listen. ■ Leads discussion after radio broadcast.	$77[d]

a. Data for India and Colombia are for 1994, data for Peru and Chile for 1985.
b. In 1985 prices. Ratio of costs to minimum wage is 1:14, and ratio of costs to per capita gross national product (GNP) is 1:40.
c. Excludes the estimated value of the in-kind contributions from beneficiary communities.
d. In 1985 prices. Ratio of costs to minimum wage is 1:5, and ratio of costs to per capita gross domestic product (GDP) is 1:18.
Source: 1994 data are from Wilson 1995; 1985 data are from Myers 1995.

in Colombia's Community Child Care and Nutrition Project, for instance, are expected to contribute on a sliding scale according to family income. In Bolivia's Integrated Child Development Project, parents pay a flat monthly fee equivalent to US$2.50 (in 1993 prices) for the first child and a decreasing fee for each additional child enrolled.

Innovative funding schemes. Thailand has worked out a funding scheme in which loans paid back to village loan funds (financed by the Christian Children's Fund) are funneled into a capital fund to support early child development programs in the community on a continuing basis.

In Mauritius the government created the Export Processing Zone Welfare Fund as a concession to EPZ workers, who make up 20 percent of the country's labor force but do not benefit from the more advantageous labor regulations that apply outside the zones. Created to finance social services for EPZ workers and their children, the fund derives its revenues from a tripartite system of monthly payments from the state, employees, and employers. The EPZ social service fund gives start-up and operating grants to nongovernmental organizations to create and run day care centers and subsidizes preschool fees for the children of EPZ workers. Under this tripartite funding system, the national government contributes about 10 percent of EPZ social service fund revenues.

PART II

The Practice

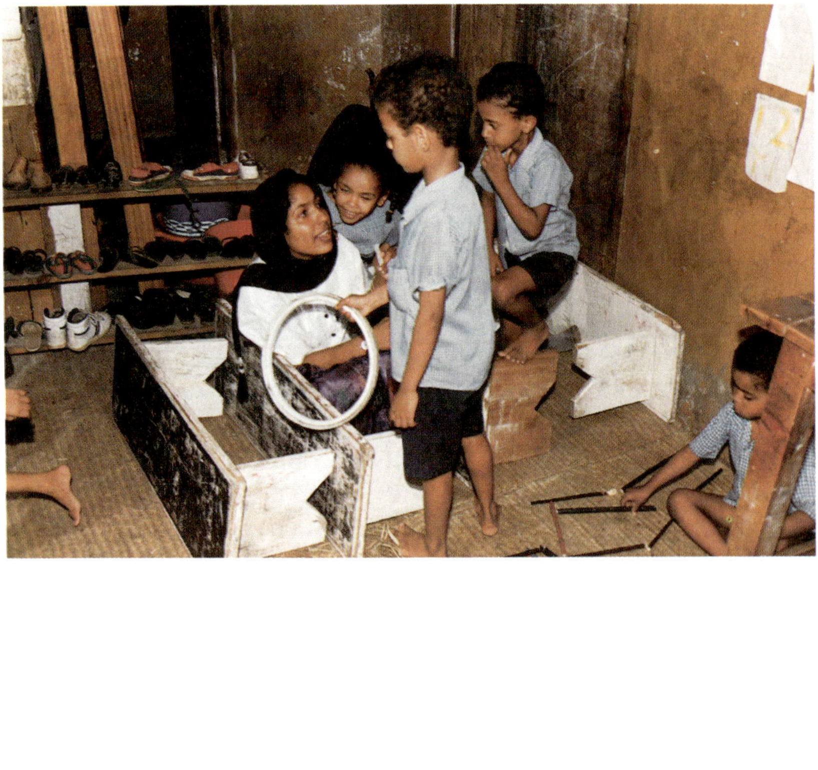

Introduction

There is now a need for reliable and valid information about what works, why it works, for whom it works, and under what conditions it works.

– Raymond Collins and others (1990, p. 18)

The mounting body of evidence that early childhood intervention can result in substantial future gains has prompted many nations to incorporate preschool programs into their national and regional development agendas. There is rising interest in these countries in nonformal models of education and care. It is thus not surprising to find programs based on the nonformal community development model operating in India (Integrated Child Development Services), Colombia (the *hogares comunitarios*, or home-based day care centers), Kenya (the Harambees, or "Let's Pull Together" movement), Brazil (*crèches comunitarias*, or community nurseries), Jamaica (the Community Study program, or backyard nurseries), the United Kingdom (Playground Movement), and Venezuela (the *hogares de cuidado diario*, or home day care program).

Because differences in cultural and economic environments make it impossible to rely on just one approach in early child development, it is important to identify a range of effective models rather than emphasize a single program model.

This section describes different programs that countries have used to promote children's physical and mental development. The interventions are grouped in five major types.

Educating Parents

Parents are children's earliest teachers, and studies have proved that strengthening mothers' ability to stimulate their children and encourage them to learn can set the stage for adult success. In an attempt to lessen the imbalances caused by poverty from the start of life, several countries have introduced national programs to train poor parents in the principles of early child development.

1. Training Children's First Teachers in Israel
2. Helping Parents Care for the Very Young in Israel

3. Searching for the Best Care Model in Turkey
4. Community Educators Working with Parents in Mexico

Training Caregivers

It is erroneously assumed that anyone can take care of young children, despite the growing wealth of research confirming the importance of teacher training to the quality of the early childhood experience. Moreover, teachers are far too often regarded as custodians and dispensers of knowledge who must follow a centrally controlled curriculum regardless of local conditions or the efficacy of other forms of learning. Instead, teachers should be trained to distinguish aspects of the curriculum that can and should be changed to accommodate local customs from those that cannot be modified without seriously compromising the program's efficacy.

5. Expanding Teacher Training Programs in Trinidad and Tobago
6. Introducing New Teaching Approaches in the Former East Bloc
7. Meeting the Increasing Need for Child Care in Kenya

Delivering Services to Children

Industrial nations have explored ways to help their poorer citizens get a better start in life for the past thirty years. Much of what they have learned can be used by early child development programs everywhere. An important lesson is that social deficits must be simultaneously attacked on several fronts: nutrition, health care, and education. This lesson underlies the U.S. Head Start program and the Special Supplementation Nutrition Program for Women and Infant Children (WIC). Programs in developing countries that deliver integrated services on a massive scale to help poor children flourish as they grow, such as India's Integrated Child Development Services and Colombia's Community Child Care and Nutrition Project, recognize this lesson as well.

8. Giving Children a Head Start in the United States
9. WIC—Preventing Low-Birth-Weight-Babies in the United States
10. Community Centers Saving Children in India
11. Rationalizing Kazakstan's Kindergarten System
12. Expanding Services for Children in Guyana
13. Planning to Meet the Needs of Children in the Philippines

Reforming Formal Education Systems to Include Preschoolers

Preschool education has been shown to enhance children's later progress and performance in school. It is positively associated with reduced repetition and dropout rates, and therefore with lower education costs. Not surprisingly, improving access to preschools is becoming a common feature of education reform.

14. Experimenting with New Service Models in Chile
15. Restoring Services for Children in El Salvador
16. Addressing Basic Health and Education Needs in Venezuela

Educating through the Mass Media

Because traditional early child interventions reach relatively few children and most innovative techniques have yet to be extended beyond the pilot stage, early education specialists are increasingly turning to the mass media to get their message out. Teaching videos in particular have great potential to convey active learning strategies—immediately, engagingly, and accurately—on a large scale. These videos can be broadcast over national television and used in training courses, health care centers, and parental discussion groups. Better-informed parents are far more likely to demand preschool enrichment services from their government and to use active learning techniques with their children at home.

17. Tuning in to Learn about Child Care in the Philippines
18. Using Radio to Teach Caregivers and Kids in Bolivia
19. Producing TV for Tots in Nigeria

1. Training Children's First Teachers in Israel

Israel's Home Instruction Program for Preschool Youngsters trains mothers from disadvantaged families to act as home teachers for their preschool-age children. Using specially designed teaching materials and workbooks, the program serves 6,000 at-risk families a year and has been found to improve cognitive development and achievement and to decrease participants' chances of dropping out of school.

Since 1969 the Hebrew University has been administering a unique home-based preschool enrichment program for disadvantaged Israeli children. Dr. Avima D. Lombard of the university's Research Institute for Innovation in Education came up with the Home Instruction Program for Preschool Youngsters (HIPPY) in order to test whether mothers trained to provide specially designed lessons to their preschoolers could improve their children's learning patterns.

HIPPY provides participating mothers of children aged three to six with educational training and materials in language development, sensory and perceptual discrimination, and problem solving. Twice a month a paraprofessional aide visits each mother in her home to deliver new storybooks and activity packets. The aide uses role playing to instruct the mother in the use of the materials, with the mother and aide taking turns playing mother and child. If the mother is illiterate, an older sibling may assume the teaching role in the mother's presence.

Mothers are expected to work with their children for a specified amount of time each week to complete the packet of programmed home activities supplied by the aide. Each activity lasts five to ten minutes, and each week's program consists of ten activity units. The degree of difficulty and pacing are carefully graduated over the course of the program. Every two weeks, the ten to fifteen HIPPY mothers supervised by the aide come together to review new lessons, share information, and offer suggestions based on their own experiences. During the meetings the women discuss such topics as health, hygiene, child development, children's books and games, the school system, handicrafts, home economics, and preparations for holidays.

HIPPY participants strengthen their own and their children's language skills by reading simple storybooks and completing detailed worksheets about content, vocabulary, and concepts that are incorporated into games and exercises. The worksheets also guide the mothers in activities aimed at developing their children's sensory discrimination skills by doing visual, auditory, and tactile exercises with simple materials and game pieces. Problem-solving activities include listing, sorting, matching, and grouping by attribute and theme.

HIPPY, studied extensively since its inception, has been shown to have a positive effect on the social, emotional, and cognitive development of preschool children. After three years of participation, HIPPY children score significantly higher than control group children on all measures of cognitive development and achievement and are far less likely to drop out of school. The effects of educational day care combined with HIPPY participation, moreover, appear to be additive. In addition, mothers who participate are accorded a higher status within the family, and their general outlook appears to be much more optimistic than that of mothers not in the program.

In 1975 Israel's Ministry of Education and Culture incorporated HIPPY into the package of education welfare services offered to localities with a high proportion of educationally disadvantaged children. The government is now committed to covering the costs of this national program and also provides the administrative infrastructure at the community level. Although one-on-one educational enrichment sounds expensive, three full years of HIPPY actually cost 40 percent less than one year of remedial education at the primary school level. Each family participating in HIPPY is expected to pay 30 to 50 percent of the program's cost per family, although program coordinators can reduce a family's required contribution when necessary. The remaining cost is covered by the government's general fund and through local fund-raising.

Today the Hebrew University Research Institute for Innovation in Education, where HIPPY originated, retains responsibility for monitoring and ensuring program quality. It also coordinates HIPPY on the regional and national levels, trains local and regional staff, and ensures a systematic flow of inputs. Every year roughly 6,000 Israeli families from about eighty urban and rural communities participate in HIPPY. Children in many other countries can now also benefit from the program, whose training and curriculum materials have been translated into Arabic, Dutch, English, German, Spanish, and Turkish.

2. Helping Parents Care for the Very Young in Israel

Building on their earlier success with HIPPY, Israeli researchers designed the HATAF program to extend home training for mothers of infants aged one to three. The HATAF program reaches children during the years of most rapid intellectual growth.

In 1973 Dr. Avima D. Lombard's Hebrew University team developed the Home Activities for Toddlers and Their Families (HATAF) program to complement the training offered by their earlier successful program, HIPPY. Based on the ideas that the home environment shapes the child and that most parents are ready and willing to improve their own skills, the HATAF program has five major goals:

- *Enrich the language skills of both mother and child.* HATAF mothers are instructed in uses of language that encourage children to talk and develop basic language concepts as they play.
- *Develop mothers' sensitivity to their toddlers' needs.* HATAF mothers are instructed about the different stages of children's development and the conditions deemed optimal at each stage. (Between the ages of one and three, for instance, children learn mainly through physical, verbal, and emotional exploration and experimentation.) The HATAF program gives mothers an idea of what to expect at each stage and a sense of the important role of adults in advancing toddlers' development.
- *Improve mothers' skills in using natural learning settings in the home.* Studies have shown that when mothers use daily events and activities as they occur to teach their children—teaching "on the fly"—their children develop a greater awareness of their environment and perform at a higher level socially, emotionally, and intellectually. The HATAF program strives to develop this skill in mothers by showing them how to turn daily occurrences and familiar situations into exploratory and learning activities for their children.
- *Refine mothers' use of reinforcement techniques.* Too much or indiscriminate use of reinforcement dilutes this powerful teaching technique's value as a spur to learning. HATAF mothers are taught to use immediate positive reinforcement in ways that are both specific and appropriate.
- *Teach parents educationally productive techniques for playing with children aged one to three.* Recent studies have confirmed the importance of

toys and play in promoting children's early development. The HATAF program shows parents how to promote learning by selecting play activities appropriate to their children's stage of development and skill level and presenting these activities in an attractive way. It also urges parents to allow adequate time and space for their children to explore and discover by themselves—now known to be the basis of learning.

To reach these goals, the HATAF program emphasizes the importance of mother-child interaction and the use of simple, inexpensive teaching materials. Typically, one professional coordinator serves sixty to eighty families in a HATAF program. The coordinators are university educated, have experience in early childhood education, and are trained intensively in HATAF methods. The HATAF program coordinators meet regularly with the HATAF national director. In addition, four to six paraprofessional home visitors, recommended by local health and social service workers, are chosen from among the mothers of older children in the target community. Home visitors are expected to be literate. Each year begins with a week of training for home visitors in early education, child growth and development, and the methods and content of the HATAF program. Additional weekly training is provided over the course of the program. Home visitors are paid according to the number of families they serve.

Each home visitor works with twelve to fourteen mothers, for about an hour a week in the first year and an hour every two weeks in the second year. Children must be no more than eleven to thirteen months old when they are enrolled in the program. Home instruction centers on new, repeated, and spontaneous play activities. The aide involves the mother in all activities to help her learn new play behaviors. Groups of fifteen to twenty area mothers meet with the professional coordinator every two or three weeks to discuss such common parenting problems as sibling rivalry, toilet training, and discipline. Periodic mother-child workshops allow mothers to see how their children interact in a group setting, and meetings are often held in health or community centers to reinforce the link between the HATAF program and other community services.

HATAF activities can be divided into eight broad areas: language enrichment, storybook reading, make-believe, eye-hand coordination, gross motor activity, sorting, memory, and transformation of materials (such as cooking). Each activity is described on written worksheets and explained by the aide. Teaching materials are either easily found in the home (shopping baskets, kitchen utensils, natural materials) or are given to the mother during the instruction period (books, balls, dolls).

Today the HATAF program serves roughly 2,000 families through twenty-five centers throughout Israel. These families pay a modest monthly fee to cover part of the cost of the materials distributed. Coordinators and aides are local employees, but the national program staff are part of the Hebrew University's Research Institute for Innovation in Education.

A 1980 study concluded that HATAF mothers are more knowledgeable than mothers not in the program about their children's development and the educational value of different activities. They are also more inclined to see themselves as active agents in their children's development. A 1989 study confirmed that HATAF mothers take a far more active role than other mothers in creating an enriching home environment for their children.

3. Searching for the Best Care Model in Turkey

In an effort to discover the best approach to caring for young children, Turkey's Early Enrichment Project conducted a study of children in custodial care, educational day care, and home care settings where half the mothers participated in training and half did not. The project found that educational day care produced the best results on all measures of psychosocial development, and that training mothers through enrichment programs involving extensive group discussions on child-rearing and maternal support was beneficial.

From 1982 to 1986 Turkey's Early Enrichment Project, seeking the optimal combination of home-based and center-based custodial and educational day care services for very young children, studied the effects of different approaches on preschool-age children. It then trained half the caregivers in each setting in early child development learning techniques and compared the results. While educational day care got the best results in all measures of psychosocial development, the children whose mothers had received training and outside support also showed significant gains (Kagitcibasi, Sunar, and Bekman 1988).

The Early Enrichment Project study evaluated child care settings in several low-income areas of Istanbul, tracking the progress of 255 children aged three to five in a variety of custodial day care, educational day care, and home care situations. Two-thirds of the mothers in the sample were factory workers with minimal education.

In the first year the study collected baseline data on the children's cognitive, social, and emotional development. All mothers were interviewed at home, and children were tested and observed both at home and in day care. In the second and third years, half of the mothers, selected randomly from each group, were trained in early child development techniques and supplied with educational materials based on the HIPPY model and adapted for Turkish use. The Turkish Mother Enrichment Program also trained the mothers selected on how to be more sensitive to their preschoolers' needs and how to foster their social, personal, and cognitive development. Training was given by paraprofessionals during biweekly home visits, and group meetings were held on alternate weeks.

The project continually built up its database. From its second year, when the five-year-olds entered school, it collected school grades at the end of every semester. In its fourth and final year, it administered a wide range of tests covering different areas of development to measure the effectiveness of the training. Tests were administered several times to increase their validity, baseline assessments were repeated in the fourth year, and school data were considered in the final evaluation.

Educational day care, it was found, produced superior results for virtually all indicators of psychosocial development, especially for cognitive development and school achievement. But children whose mothers received training also surpassed those in the control group in every measure. It was also found that trained mothers were treated with greater respect by their families, talked more and showed greater responsiveness when dealing with their children, and had higher aspirations for the future. The study concluded that parental education—less costly than center-based care—is effective and is well suited for wide application in Turkey, particularly when integrated into existing health and nutrition education programs.

In 1992, six years after the completion of the four-year study, a follow-up study was carried out to assess the long-term effects of training mothers. Of the original 255 families, 217 participated. The follow-up entailed extensive interviews with the young participants (now adolescents), with mothers and some fathers, and assessments of adolescents' school performance and intellectual competence. It was found that more of the participants whose mothers had received training were still in school. The children also tested higher in language use, mathematics, and overall academic performance during the five years of primary school and had larger vocabularies (as measured by a standardized test). Both the adolescents whose mothers had had training and their parents were generally more positive about the children's level of social integration, personal autonomy, academic orientation, and school adjustment than were members of the control group. They also reported better family relations and a higher status for mothers.

These results indicate that enriching the preschool experience confers substantial long-term benefits. In an effort organized by the Mother-Child Foundation and the Adult Education Division of the Ministry of Education and supported by a World Bank loan, the education methods devised and tested by Turkey's Early Enrichment Project are now being disseminated on a national scale.

4. Community Educators Working with Parents in Mexico

In an effort to enhance the early experience of Mexico's poorest infants, the national Initial Education Project is sending community educators into the home to teach parents what they can do to help their children develop. Early response to the project has been enthusiastic, and under its influence many of the country's traditional child-rearing practices are giving way to change.

In 1992 Mexico's Ministry of Education—in cooperation with UNESCO, UNDP, UNICEF, and the World Bank—launched a five-year Initial Education Project to improve the child care techniques used by the parents of 1.2 million of the country's poorest children under the age of three. The community educators who deliver the message are the keystone of the project. Generally young parents themselves or health providers living in the community, educators receive a stipend of US$150 a month. Their training consists of a two-week preservice course plus monthly follow-up sessions. Educators are expected to instruct parents about child development, positive parenting practices, nutrition, basic health and hygiene, and family planning.

In addition to organizing periodic group sessions, community educators visit parents in their homes once a week or every other week to teach them how to care for and stimulate their children in ways that will encourage the children's cognitive, psychological, and social development. By June 1995, 174,800 parents had undergone training in parenting, and it is estimated that 900,000 parents will be reached over the five-year life of the project.

The project has created jobs for 12,000 community educators, each of whom works with twenty families at a time. Ten of these community "nuclei" make up a "module," which receives technical input from a module supervisor. Ten modules form a "zone," monitored by a zone coordinator. Because Mexico's health and education services are handled by different ministries, the project was not designed to include a health component. Nevertheless, the coordination of these services has been excellent, with community educators and local health committees frequently conducting joint meetings for the local community to discuss child care and development issues.

Parents report that the training has changed their attitudes about child-rearing, and many say they now recognize that traditional punishments for children are often inappropriate and unnecessary. In some areas the program is also changing ideas about gender roles in child-rearing. In remote villages in Chiapas, for instance, it is fathers who attend the training sessions.

5. Expanding Teacher Training Programs in Trinidad and Tobago

Trinidad and Tobago, as part of its Basic Education Project, is working with the private organization Servol and the University of the West Indies to expand the educational opportunities open to preschool program managers. The project will also train 350 current and 300 new preschool teachers and supervise them on the job.

Trinidad and Tobago, with Bank support, has undertaken to improve the quality of basic education throughout the country, and upgrading preschool programs is part of that campaign.

Two major institutions certify preschool teachers in Trinidad and Tobago—Servol, a nongovernmental organization that runs 148 government-funded child care centers in the country, and the University of the West Indies. Servol's two-year preschool training program includes one year of full-time study and one year of supervised apprenticeship in the classroom. The University of the West Indies offers a six-month course in methodology and another six-month course in the management of early childhood centers. The Basic Education Project is strengthening and expanding these programs to train the trainers and will also sponsor workshops for field supervisors run by Servol, other NGOs, and the Ministry of Education.

The Basic Education Project's preschool trainer and supervisor training program focuses on curriculum content and training strategies. To allow participants to gain new knowledge while continuing in their jobs, it will offer seven one-week training sessions over the course of a year. On the job, participants will form teams to observe and comment on one another's performance. During the training sessions, consultants will provide feedback on participants' performance and teach them how to run workshops, how to offer helpful comments to other teachers, and how to implement a preschool curriculum. They will assess participants both at work and during the workshops the participants prepare and show them how to make safe, effective teaching equipment from such common items as shells, bottle caps, plastic scraps, old newspapers, and discarded lumber.

The project will also fund up to 350 scholarships for preservice training for prospective preschool teachers and give additional stipends to trainees from low-income communities during their year of full-time training. Servol will conduct field workshops so that roughly 130 teachers presently employed in early childhood programs can receive pre-service training certification. In addition, each regional division of the Ministry of Education will have experts in early childhood care and education work with NGOs in training, supervising, and supporting in-service teacher trainees.

6. Introducing New Teaching Approaches in the Former East Bloc

The dramatic change in the countries of Eastern Europe and the former Soviet Union extends even to the kindergarten classroom. In line with the move toward democracy and a market economy, the Soros Foundation is sponsoring a project to train kindergarten teachers in educational approaches that encourage individuality and choice making.

One of the better legacies of communism is the high-quality kindergarten system ranging across all countries of the former Eastern Bloc. These are clean, safe places where working parents can leave their preschool-age children with confidence—from 7 a.m. to 7 p.m. Many of these facilities remain in good condition, so heavy investment in new child care centers is unnecessary. Less heartening is the old communist preschool curriculum, which takes no account of the special developmental needs of young children. Teachers tend to use the lecture approach and to require all children to do the same thing at the same time.

Under the Soros Child Development Program, teachers in seventeen formerly communist countries (Albania, Belarus, Bulgaria, Croatia, the Czech Republic, Estonia, the former Yugoslav Republic of Macedonia, Hungary, the Kyrgyz Republic, Lithuania, Moldova, Russia, Romania, the Slovak Republic, Slovenia, Ukraine, and Yugoslavia) are learning the best early child education techniques used in the United States and Western Europe. The program's curriculum, designed by Children's Resources International (CRI), emphasizes child-initiated play balanced by opportunities for group learning. The project funds teacher training and the purchase of materials for classrooms (books, paints, paper, substances that can be manipulated, wooden blocks, sandboxes, and water tables).

At the end of 1993 each of the Soros Foundation's country offices hired two local people to staff the country's child development program. In January 1994 these staff members and selected teachers attended a six-week training course in child-centered learning techniques in the United States. Visiting many Head Start and other early child development programs, they observed the techniques in practice and learned to distinguish between excellent programs and those of lower quality. To give continued support, CRI provides ongoing technical assistance, and its trainers make follow-up visits to each country.

After the first year of operation, CRI-trained teachers began to train new teachers.

Kindergartens participate only with the agreement of the ministry of education. Each is encouraged to adapt the basic curriculum as it sees fit and continues to be responsible for paying its teachers' salaries. Thus, even if a country stops participating in the program, the benefits and basic care-giving structure remain.

Participating preschools are required to use a child-centered curriculum that teaches children to make choices as they play and gives each child an individual learning experience. Parents, too, must participate, and each site is encouraged to establish a "parents' room"—stocked with coffee, snacks, and sometimes even a washing machine—where parents can gather. Parents and grandparents also participate as salaried or volunteer teachers' aides, a feature that required legal changes in some countries. The Soros program sees the energy and enthusiasm of the newly involved parents as one of the most positive aspects of its preschool program.

The cost per child has varied widely depending on a country's resources. In Moldova the cost in the first year was US$157 a child. In Croatia and Albania it was as high as US$600 a child. But in the second year, Moldova's costs fell to US$20 a child, with start-up costs and reusable materials already paid for. Parents' contributions, though uniformly modest, also vary from country to country.

The positive response to the preschool program throughout the region has prompted CRI to begin work on a curriculum for infants and toddlers. And to ensure that gains made in preschool are not lost once the children enter the formal education system, a first-grade curriculum based on active learning principles will be introduced in 1996 by the countries participating in the Soros Child Development Program.

7. Meeting the Increasing Need for Child Care in Kenya

As more women enter the workforce in Kenya, the demand for early child development services has skyrocketed. To find out how best to improve and expand services, the government is launching a pilot early child development project with support from the World Bank.

In Kenya today, roughly half the country's 6 million preschool-age children live in poverty, a third of households are headed by women, and more and more women are entering the workforce. Not surprisingly, the demand for quality child care is rising. As a first step toward meeting this demand, the government—with World Bank assistance—has initiated a pilot early child development project.

Kenya already has a substantial network of community-supported preschool facilities, with some 18,400 centers caring for roughly a million children aged three to six. The communities provide the facilities, pay caregivers, organize the children's food programs, and supply materials for learning and play. The national government funds the training of preschool teacher trainers and designs the preschool curriculum. District governments train teachers and inspect and evaluate programs. And NGOs and local governments give financial and supervisory support to some centers. But with no recognized standards, preschool programs vary significantly in quality and type.

A recent government evaluation of the preschool system identified several weaknesses:

- Access to services—particularly for the poor—was low.
- The quality of physical facilities, personnel, services, and activities varied widely.
- With increasing numbers of children under age three attending child care centers and no plan in place for dealing with them during these crucial years, the risk of impaired early development was high.
- The public was largely unaware of the importance of early child development services.
- Caregivers' wages varied widely, and payment was irregular.
- Monitoring and supervision were inadequate.
- Preschool programs were not linked to the primary school system.
- Funding levels were too low to support efficient and effective preschool programs.

Kenya's pilot project will test ways of improving the quality of early child development services, increasing access for poor children, and increasing communities' capacity to organize, manage, and finance programs. It will also develop and test broader packages of services. To measure the pilot's success, the program will monitor poor children's access to early child development programs, profiles of children on entering primary school (average age, height, weight, immunization status), and dropout and repetition rates in the early grades.

The project proposes to train 15,000 preschool teachers and 5,000 community representatives on how to run and monitor enriched child care programs. To improve preschoolers' health and nutrition, the project will offer immunizations and food and micronutrient supplements and monitor growth. Pilot preschools will employ staff capable of diagnosing and treating common ailments, deworming children, and referring more severe cases for higher levels of care. Centers will continue to be managed by parents committees trained in the organization, management, and monitoring of early child services. An operations manual will outline targeting, disbursement, accounting, and auditing methods, and grants will be given to some communities to improve services. NGOs will help oversee the communities' management of child care centers.

The project will introduce new ways for communities to finance teachers' salaries, subsidize fees for the poorest children (in some cases, it will give grants directly to poor children to enable them to attend preschool), purchase school supplies, provide health and education materials, and improve facilities. It will also test a primary school curriculum that continues the teaching methods begun in preschool.

8. Giving Children a Head Start in the United States

In the mid-1960s the United States, as part of its War on Poverty, launched Project Head Start to provide education, health, and social services to the country's neediest preschool-age children. One of the first examples of an integrated early child development program, Head Start has served some 14.6 million youngsters. But because of inconsistent quality, its impact has been difficult to assess.

Head Start is a comprehensive early child development program providing education, health, and social services to low-income children and their families. Begun in the summer of 1965 as an eight-week demonstration project, Head Start became an essential element of President Johnson's War on Poverty. From its inception Head Start recognized the need to address children's educational, physical, and social service needs holistically—and to extend help to their families and communities as well. Head Start programs have four goals, each overseen by a different local coordinator, who makes sure that services meet the project's performance standards:

- *Education.* To provide each child with age-appropriate learning experiences that foster intellectual, social, and emotional growth.
- *Health.* To provide a comprehensive program of immunizations and medical, dental, mental health, and nutrition services.
- *Social services.* To help families assess their needs, gain access to services, and build on family strengths.
- *Parental involvement.* To instruct parents in caregiving and teaching techniques and to encourage them to volunteer in the classroom and to plan and manage preschool programs.

Over the past thirty years Head Start has served about 14.6 million children and their families. In 1994 alone it served 740,493 children, in more than 40,000 classrooms operated by 1,405 grantees. In 1993, 12 percent of its local sponsors were school systems or local government agencies, 47 percent were community action agencies (federally supported service delivery entities), and 28 percent were private nonprofit agencies.

Yet because of inadequate federal funding, the program today serves only 30 percent of eligible children—those whose families have incomes at or below the federal poverty guideline (US$15,150 for a family of four) or are eligible for public assistance. (Only about 5 percent of participants have incomes below the requirement, and about 13 percent of participants are disabled.) Moreover, because of inadequate funding, most children enter Head Start when they are four years old, despite growing evidence that earlier intervention is more effective. In 1994 Head Start initiated the Early Head Start Program to provide early, continuous, and comprehensive child development and family support services to low-income families and their children up to age three.

In 1993 the federal cost per child for the program ranged from US$3,500 to US$6,000, averaging US$4,343. In 1992 federal funds for the local programs were allocated as follows: 41 percent for education, 13 percent for administration, 13 percent for site occupancy, 9 percent for health and nutrition, 8 percent for transportation, 5 percent for social services, 4 percent to stimulate parent involvement, 3 percent for disability services, and 4 percent for other costs. Communities are required to match 20 percent of federal funds, in cash or in kind. In fiscal 1995 the federal appropriation for Head Start was US$3.5 billion.

The vast majority of Head Start children attend center-based, part-day programs during the school year only. Two home visits are required over the course of the program. The cost per child for home-based programs, in which a Head Start worker comes to the child's home weekly to work intensively with the parents, is about 10 to 20 percent less than that for center-based programs. Families can choose to combine the center-based and home-based approaches.

Head Start requires that classrooms be staffed by two paid staff persons—a teacher and a teacher's aide or two teachers. The program also tries to have a third person, a volunteer, in the classroom at all times. The Head Start staff-to-child ratio is capped at 1:10, and the average classroom has about seventeen children. In 1994 fewer than half of Head Start teachers had undergraduate or advanced degrees. More had child development associate degrees earned through a combination of classroom and in-service training, for which scholarships are federally funded. The 1994 Head Start reauthorization bill strengthened the program's staff requirements so that by 1996 each classroom will be required to have a teacher who meets specific early child education training requirements.

Evaluations of Head Start over the years (McCall 1993) have found that it produces:

- Improvements in IQ scores and in academic readiness and achievement, greater self-esteem, and better social behavior and health.
- Better high school attendance rates, reduced retention in grade, and less use of special education services.
- Better communication between parents and children, increased parental participation in school programs, improved disciplinary practices in the home, and fewer feelings of anxiety and depression.
- Greater parental involvement in the child's early education, which was significantly associated with the child's later academic success.

- Improvement in the community attitude toward the poor and toward services for the poor.
- Substantial employment opportunities for the poor (36 percent of the program's employees are Head Start parents or former students; Children's Defense Fund 1993).

Head Start's greatest problems have been inconsistent program quality and the tendency for preschoolers' gains to fade by the time they reach the third grade. There has been no national longitudinal study of Head Start comparable to the High/Scope Perry Preschool longitudinal study, which suggested a US$7.16 return on every US$1.00 invested in early child development (Schweinhart, Barnes, and Weikart 1993). Because of the broad flexibility afforded local programs and the diversity of participants, Head Start is difficult to assess in a large study. It cannot be regarded as a uniform "treatment" and must be assessed for multiple outcomes in terms of its multiple goals (Collins and others 1990). Future Head Start evaluations need to focus on discovering what elements have proved most effective and how to ensure better-quality programs nationwide.

9. WIC—Preventing Low-Birth-Weight Babies in the United States

The U.S. WIC program provides supplemental food, nutrition education, health care, and breastfeeding counseling to low-income women deemed to be nutritionally at risk and to their children up to age five. Operating for more than thirty years, WIC has cut the incidence of very low-birth-weight babies in the United States by 44 percent and the rate of late fetal death by a third. Every dollar invested in prenatal WIC saves US$1.92 to US$4.21 in averted Medicaid costs.

After the 1969 White House Conference on Food, Nutrition, and Health, the U.S. government established the Special Supplemental Nutrition Program for Women, Infants, and Children (WIC) to provide supplemental food, nutrition education, health care, and breastfeeding counseling to low-income, nutritionally at-risk pregnant and post-partum women and their children up to age five. The program has proved to be one of the most efficient ways to improve America's health.

To qualify for WIC, a client must meet certain income criteria and be certified as nutritionally at risk by a WIC clinic or doctor. States may set their income criterion no higher than 185 percent of the federal poverty level and no lower than the federal poverty level (Jones and Richardson 1995). Nutritional risk is determined on the basis of weight, height, and a blood test. Women taking part in WIC typically suffer from anemia, weight problems, preeclampsia, chronic infections, alcohol or drug abuse, homelessness, or mental retardation. Many have a history of low-birth-weight babies, premature births, or neonatal loss. Children in the program exhibit signs of anemia, low birth weight, failure to thrive, lead poisoning, stunting, chronic infections, and congenital malformations. The nutritional risk status of all participants is recertified at regular intervals.

WIC has four components: a food package, nutrition education, medical care, and breastfeeding counseling. The WIC nutritionist gives each new WIC client vouchers redeemable for food items needed to correct that client's particular nutritional deficits. There are seven different food packages, but each usually includes milk or cheese, dry beans and peas or peanut butter, iron-fortified cereal, fruit or vegetable juice containing vitamin C, infant cereal, and infant formula. The average value of the food package is US$30 a month. The frequency with which coupons are issued varies from state to state (New York, for instance, issues coupons every two months).

While issuing food vouchers, the WIC nutritionist discusses good nutrition with clients, each of whom is required to attend at least two nutrition education sessions during her six-month certification. Meetings with the WIC counselor also provide an opportunity for pregnant participants to receive prenatal medical care. The improved birth outcomes for WIC participants can be attributed largely to early and frequent care during their pregnancies (box 11). One-on-one interaction with a caring professional is viewed by many as the key to the program's success.

Whenever possible, WIC clinics are located in a public or private nonprofit health agency that can provide ongoing, routine pediatric and obstetric care. Some programs have also had great success with mobile clinics, which pay regular, scheduled visits to at-risk neighborhoods.

Box 11 What WIC does

Prenatal

Reduces infant mortality rates

Reduced late fetal death rate by 20 to 33 percent.

Improves pregnancy outcomes

Significantly increased infant head size.

Reduced number of premature births to white women by 23 percent and to black women by 15 percent.

Reduced number of low-birth-weight births by 25 percent and of very low-birth-weight births by 44 percent.

Improves children's development

Associated with higher vocabulary test scores for children.

Women

Improves diets

WIC women consumed more iron, protein, calcium, and vitamin C than nonparticipants.

Infants and children

Improves children's diets

WIC infants consumed more iron and vitamin C than nonparticipants.

WIC children consumed more iron, vitamin C, thiamin, and niacin than nonparticipants.

Improves children's health

Rates of childhood anemia fell 16 percent after six months of WIC.

Reduced children's anemia rate nationwide by two-thirds between 1975 and 1985.

Improves children's development

WIC children tested higher than nonparticipants for digit memory.

Source: Based on Rush and others 1988; Yip 1987; GAO 1992.

To encourage breastfeeding, WIC offers more generous food packages to nursing mothers. Programs also hire lactation specialists or paraprofessionals trained to work with mothers, produce instructional materials, and buy breastpumps to lend to working mothers.

Studies over the years have consistently found the U.S. Special Supplemental Nutrition Program for Women, Infants, and Children to be a cost-effective way to improve the nation's health and to target services to Americans most in need. It has been estimated that for every dollar spent on prenatal care, US$1.92 to US$4.21 in Medicaid costs for mothers and newborns is averted. (For major studies of the past decade, see Rush and others 1988; GAO 1992; and Mathematica Policy Research 1990, 1991, 1992, and 1993.)

10. Community Centers Saving Children in India

India's community centers, or anganwadis, *serve about 16 million children a year in the largest child development program in the world. Yet the program will have to expand still further if the country is to meet its great need for health and education services for women, infants, and children.*

In rural India in 1984, 124 of every thousand children born to illiterate mothers died before age one. In the same rural areas in 1991, about 64 percent of children under three exhibited some level of malnutrition. And of the 101 million Indian children enrolled in primary school in 1991–92, 47 percent dropped out.

To improve the lot of its poor children, the Indian government initiated Integrated Child Development Services (ICDS) in 1975. ICDS has been supported by the World Food Programme, CARE, UNICEF, the European Union, USAID, and the World Bank. The World Bank has approved two loans in support of ICDS; the first supports the program in the states of Andhra Pradesh and Orissa, the second in the states of Madhya Pradesh and Bihar. The first loan was approved in 1990 and is to close in 1997; the second was approved in 1993 and is to close in 2000.

The program, now in virtually all Indian states, offers supplementary nutrition (usually hot meals of lentils, rice, and vegetables, or a mixture of grains) for children up to six and for pregnant and nursing women. For three- to six-year-olds, it offers preschool education, immunizations, health checkups, and medical referral services. For pregnant and lactating women, it offers health and nutrition education.

ICDS services are delivered through a network of *anganwadi* (courtyard) centers, each run by an *anganwadi* worker and a helper selected from the local village. The *anganwadi* workers provide nonformal preschool education, supplementary feeding, health and nutrition education, parenting education, and maternal and child health referrals. They are paid an honorarium of US$7.50 to US$10.80 a month, depending on their educational qualifications.

One of the program's greatest challenges has been to provide training to its many workers. Some *anganwadis* are established two years before the workers can receive training. And some workers are able to weigh children correctly, for instance, but unable to plot growth charts or interpret the charts to advise mothers about future care. Improving program consistency and worker training is essential.

The two Bank-supported projects are designed to improve the delivery of supplementary foods, the coordination of health and nutrition services, the training of *anganwadi* workers, and the supply of preschool educational toys and materials. They also promote the introduction of interactive learning techniques. Each of the projects has established targets, by state, for reductions in severe malnutrition, moderate malnutrition, and infant mortality. In an effort to take the needs of the whole child into account, the projects aim to improve services for all age groups, but particularly for women and adolescent girls.

A recent review of nearly thirty nutritional impact studies confirmed that the ICDS program has had a positive impact on children under six. A 1984–86 comparative study found higher infant mortality rates in non-ICDS areas, and a study on the effects on primary education found that ICDS participants had higher primary school enrollment rates and better attendance and performance records. ICDS children from low- and middle-caste groups also had significantly lower primary school dropout rates than non-ICDS children from those groups (Consultative Group on Early Childhood Care and Development 1993).

11. Rationalizing Kazakstan's Kindergarten System

With the restructuring and privatization of state-owned enterprises, responsibility for kindergartens in Kazakstan is being passed on to municipalities, which can ill afford to operate them. At the same time tough economic conditions mean that young families must have two salaries to survive, making the need for a rational kindergarten system ever more pressing.

In the newly independent Republic of Kazakstan neither revenue-strapped municipal governments nor enterprises in the process of privatizing are able to provide the liberal maternity leave, subsidized child care, and free kindergarten that the population had come to regard as entitlements under the Soviet system. Under communism, about 60 percent of the appropriate age group attended kindergarten, but by the end of 1994 enrollment had fallen to less than 30 percent. This decline reflects the approximately one-third reduction in available places between 1984 and 1994, the increase in the real value of fees in the face of declining real wages, and increased unemployment among women (both by choice and for lack of jobs).

The Kazakstan Social Protection Project, financed by a World Bank loan, is attempting to find ways to deliver social services and social protection during the difficult period of economic transition. Pilot projects have been established to help municipalities in the oblasts of South Kazakstan and Pavlodar cope with the divestiture by enterprises of health clinics, hospitals, and kindergartens and to help ensure the continued provision of services. The Bank loan is also financing modest rehabilitation and upgrading and the purchase of critical supplies and equipment for selected medical and kindergarten facilities, and the cofinancing—on a declining basis—of divested facilities' recurrent costs.

The project will also help municipalities to rationalize their social service systems and make them sustainable. To cut costs, oblast and municipal governments are considering such options as amalgamating services, targeting them more precisely, privatizing nonessential services, closing excess facilities, and improving food procurement practices. And to recover costs, they are considering introducing or increasing user fees and rationalizing and enforcing fee schedules. In 1992 Kazakstan's president decreed that kindergartens could charge fees to cover up to 30 percent of food costs, but a generous fee exemption and reduction policy and a general failure to collect fees resulted in lower-than-expected revenues.

Determining the actual need for services is an essential part of rationalization. In the city of Shymkent, for instance, where fifty-seven municipal kindergartens and fifty-six enterprise kindergartens had served a population of 450,000, the project will finance the rehabilitation costs of the seventy-seven kindergartens deemed necessary. Of the rest, about twenty of the enterprise kindergartens will not be transferred to the municipality, ten kindergartens had already closed, and six municipal kindergartens housed in nonstandard buildings will be closed or converted to other uses.

By June 1995 about 23 percent of enterprise kindergartens operating in Kazakstan at the end of 1994 had closed their doors, but the promise of funding under the Social Protection Project has moved teachers and mothers at several sites to start renovating so that they can reopen the kindergartens. In some kindergartens the women have replaced walls and fixed roofs and floors.

Kazakstan, in the midst of preparing a national strategy for the divestiture of social assets and provision of social services, has yet to define the social, economic, and educational role that kindergartens will play in the new republic. Will they be day care facilities whose major purpose is to care for the children of working parents, or early child development centers that provide education, immunizations, primary medical care, and nutrition services? While the government sets quality and coverage standards for the country's early child program, the Kazakstan Social Protection Project will maintain at least a critical minimum of kindergartens in each project city.

12. Expanding Services for Children in Guyana

Despite being the second-poorest country in the world, Guyana recognizes the need to provide comprehensive services for children. With support from the World Bank, the government is combining basic health and nutrition services with center-based early education in a system to reestablish the provision of social services to the poor.

Guyana's economic troubles since its independence in 1966 illustrate well how an economy with ample natural and human resources can be devastated by counterproductive government policies. During its first twenty years the country's economy suffered from centralized decision-making, heavy public sector involvement, and a general disregard for the need to encourage the private sector. The subsequent economic decline has severely weakened once-strong social service delivery systems.

In 1988 Guyana's government—with the assistance of the International Monetary Fund (IMF) and the International Development Association (IDA)—embarked on a series of measures aimed at restoring economic growth and normalizing relations with external donors. At the same time it initiated the complementary Social Impact Amelioration Program (SIMAP).

Under the World Bank–funded Health, Nutrition, Water, and Sanitation Project, SIMAP is trying to reestablish the country's health care services and to improve the quality of existing child care facilities. The program provides food supplements to children under five and to pregnant and lactating women (one or two meals a day), rehabilitates and equips health care and day care centers, and constructs water supply and sanitation facilities and residential drainage systems. It also funds the construction, expansion, or rehabilitation of maternal and child outpatient service departments in district hospitals and provides supplies and seed stocks of essential drugs for primary health care facilities.

The program provides food supplements to all children aged six months to two years, to all malnourished children aged two to five years, and to all pregnant and lactating women visiting health clinics. The milk and rice distributed are purchased weekly by the sponsoring agency from qualified local suppliers. Evaluations suggest that free food is drawing women and children back into the health care system and that participation in "well child" clinics has increased dramatically.

Although Guyana's present system of day care centers can accommodate no more than a thousand children, even this level of commitment is unique for a country of its economic status. The day care centers are run by the municipalities, and a private day care industry is starting to develop. The government of Guyana trains all day care workers, including those working in private centers. Guyana's day care system may be limited right now, but the country clearly knows that young children are a good investment for the future.

13. Planning to Meet the Needs of Children in the Philippines

The Philippines is laying the groundwork for a massive program to improve and expand public services for young children. To establish baseline indicators and to chart the direction of funding for early child development services, it has initiated a thorough study of the current system.

At the request of the Philippines Department of Health, the World Bank and the Asian Development Bank (ADB) prepared a report in 1994 to serve as the basis for further investment in the country's integrated child development programs. The report reviewed all current programs and activities related to Philippine children's health, nutrition, and early education.

The Philippines Departments of Health, Education, Social Welfare and Development, and Culture and Sport are now using that report to prepare a national early child program. While the Philippines investment plan is still in its early stages, it will certainly cover health, nutrition, and education, pursuing these general goals:

- *Health.* Strengthening and expanding child survival programs (including immunization programs and measures to control diarrheal

Box 12 Integrated management of the sick child: the WHO-UNICEF approach

The most common health complaints for children worldwide relate to diarrhea, pneumonia, malaria, measles, and malnutrition—frequently in combination. Recognizing the complex overlap of symptoms and effects, WHO and UNICEF have developed a health care approach of looking at each child's condition as a whole rather than targeting single diseases as in the past. The World Bank's *World Development Report 1993* cited this new, integrated approach as a cost-effective health intervention for low-income and middle-income countries and predicted that it would do much to reduce the global burden of disease.

Integrated management has several basic goals:

- Accurate diagnosis in outpatient settings.
- Combined treatment of all major illnesses.
- Speedy referral for severe cases.
- Widespread promotion of such preventive interventions as immunizations, breastfeeding, and improved nutrition.

To help achieve these goals, health workers are being trained in how to assess, classify, and treat common diseases and how to instruct parents in basic health principles and practices. During training at a first-level facility, health workers will be taught to use the WHO-UNICEF case management guidelines, and some will be trained in the management of drug supplies. Integrated management treatment charts and training methods have been tested in Ethiopia and Tanzania, and monitoring and evaluation tools are being developed. The integrated management of childhood disease shows such promise that the World Bank is already collaborating with WHO to introduce it in Bank-supported projects in Brazil, the Philippines, and Tanzania.

Source: Based on information provided by Mariam Claeson, World Bank, October 1995.

and respiratory disease) and perhaps launching a targeted "sick child" initiative.

- *Nutrition.* Strengthening and expanding programs for malnourished children, promoting breastfeeding and correct infant feeding practices, and supplying micronutrient supplements to at-risk mothers and children.
- *Early education.* Strengthening and expanding public preschool programs and testing a variety of day care schemes to help working mothers.

All investment would narrowly target the poor and be designed to maximize community participation. An initial round of community interviews about the content of early child programs has already been completed, and two more rounds of consultation—and a program to mobilize local support for such programs—are planned.

Besides serving as a guide for planning, the 1994 World Bank–ADB report should also prove useful in attracting donor support. Once published, the report will be discussed at a donors workshop and distributed to potential funding sources worldwide.

Chura

14. Experimenting with New Service Models in Chile

Chile is trying to learn more about which kinds of early child development approaches are most effective in urban and rural settings. Its Primary Education Improvement Project is assessing how improving teacher training and teaching materials and providing food supplements affect poor children's futures.

In 1989 less than a fifth of all two- to five-year-olds were enrolled in preschool, and only 57.5 percent of that student cohort finished the eighth grade. To improve this record, the Chilean government in 1992 launched the Bank-assisted Primary Education Improvement Project, to provide preschool education for about 16,000 urban and 30,000 rural five-year-olds from poor families.

The project is hiring supervisors, teachers, and paraprofessionals; training parents in how to stimulate the minds of their young children; constructing 100 classrooms to provide roughly 4,500 preschool places; refurbishing 75 rural facilities donated by the communities; providing daily food for the children; providing teaching materials; instituting a mass media campaign to encourage parental participation; and conducting studies to ascertain the cost-effectiveness of each preschool model tried. Preschool programs are judged by their medium-term impact on the children's academic performance, behavior, and skills.

The project is testing two models of rural preschool education. Under the first model, the project is providing 29,000 sets of teaching materials and continuous in-service training for supervisors, school principals, teachers, and paraprofessionals. It is also conducting 3,000 local workshops to train some 23,400 parents in early education techniques. No food supplements are provided.

The second model is being implemented by INTEGRA, a government-assisted agency that was responsible for enrolling 12.4 percent of all preschoolers in 1989. INTEGRA is hiring 15 supervisors and 150 paraprofessionals, refurbishing 75 small rural centers donated by the communities, and providing 2,000 daily food rations. Each rural child care center is run by two paraprofessionals and serves about twenty-five children under the age of six.

Evaluation procedures are integrated into all preschool programs. Mechanisms are set up at the outset to assess each model's effect on children's future academic achievement, behavior, and skills, and a cost-effectiveness study will compare the three urban and two rural preschool models. These evaluations of the programs' relevance, efficiency, and effectiveness will guide future government investment in preschool expansion.

15. Restoring Services for Children in El Salvador

After years of war, El Salvador is now restoring and improving its education and health services for young children. The unique, community-based preschool system it has developed requires the active participation of parents and other community members. Improved facilities and new teaching methods and materials in the classroom are benefiting preschoolers.

During El Salvador's ten years of civil strife, an estimated 75,000 people died, 750,000 emigrated, and 500,000 became refugees within their own country. Defense spending and interest payments on external debt crowded out spending for social services, and the children suffered. In 1991 about 60 percent of infant deaths resulted from diarrhea caused by lack of adequate sanitary facilities and practices. About 36 percent of children under five suffered from vitamin A deficiency in 1988, and only 29 percent of children under two received any health care at all. On the education front, only 7 percent finished primary school in 1979, and a fifth of rural first-graders dropped out. By 1986 only 60 percent of children in rural areas were enrolled in primary school.

In June 1989 the government of El Salvador instituted a far-reaching macroeconomic reform program and, with World Bank, USAID, and UNICEF support, began to implement the Social Sector Rehabilitation Project to rebuild public sector health and education services. As part of that project, El Salvador has devised an innovative program that encourages parents and community groups to define and administer preschool and early primary education services for about 70,000 students. Each preschool will accommodate at least twenty-eight children. Using established criteria, the Ministry of Education selects a community group (formed by teachers and parents or by NGOs) to run the preschools and provides funds to cover teachers' salaries and administrative costs, textbooks and teaching materials, nutrition assistance, and staff training. The community groups are responsible for hiring and paying teachers, providing furniture and physical facilities, and administering services.

Under the program, in-service training in the theory and practice of early child development will be provided for about 2,500 preprimary teachers. The program emphasizes small-group interaction and activities that strengthen children's problem-solving skills and readiness for reading, writing, and numeracy. All preprimary teachers in El Salvador will eventually be trained through the Ministry of Education, which runs regional preschool teacher training centers.

The cost of providing preschool services under this project has been estimated at about US$120 a child per year, including US$20 for food supplements. Teachers are paid US$160 a month to teach preprimary classes; teachers with larger classes can receive a salary increase of up to 10 percent. The project includes annual evaluations of preprimary and primary programs for their effect on child development and their cost-effectiveness, which will provide a basis for refining the programs' design. It is hoped that the programs can be adapted for other high-poverty areas in El Salvador.

El Salvador's Social Sector Rehabilitation Project also supports the expansion of education and health outreach activities; seeks to increase the number of health specialists and medicines available in villages; and includes an emergency birth and first-aid service. It will strengthen the social sector by instituting a new supervision system, improving financial and personnel management practices, and developing a health care financing policy—all of which will have implications for the country's network of early child development programs.

16. Addressing Basic Health and Education Needs in Venezuela

The Venezuelan government has made a strong commitment to expanding the capacity of its community day care and preschool programs. New construction and renovation projects undertaken with World Bank support have surpassed their project goals, opening the door to preschool education for thousands of young children.

Venezuela's abundant petroleum resources have made the nation rich. Yet in June 1994 almost half of Venezuelans were considered poor and more than a fifth critically poor. In 1988 only a third of preschool-age children attended a preschool program, and access to primary school was not universal. Venezuela's skewed income distribution and heavy burden of poverty derive chiefly from poor management of the national budget, insufficient targeting of social spending on the poor, rapid urbanization, and a high rate of population growth.

In 1990, with World Bank support, the government launched a seven-year Social Development Project to rehabilitate the primary health care network; provide health care and nutrition services for pregnant and lactating women and for children up to age six; expand and improve preschool services for poor children; mount a campaign promoting beneficial health, nutrition, and education practices; and improve the government's capacity to design, plan, and implement social programs and assess their impact.

By the end of 1994 preschool programs had reached an estimated 44 percent of eligible children. The government's aim is to enroll at least half of all four- to six-year-olds in preschool programs by 1995. It is therefore supporting the establishment of new preschools, both conventional and informal. In conventional preschools young children receive formal instruction from a professional teacher. Informal preschool education in Venezuela tends to be provided by a teacher and community promoter who share teaching duties and provide health, nutrition, and recreation services.

The project will have built 1,600 conventional preschool classrooms by the end of 1995, which should accommodate 96,000 children. It will also build 185 informal preschool centers, extending coverage to 116,000 children in all. Although the construction of preschools has been highly successful, funds for building were recently cut 40 percent, and project funds must also cover the preschool feeding program, the purchase of furniture and materials, staff training and supervision, and administrative costs.

Community day care programs, expanded under the project, now serve 351,000 children and should easily reach the target of 500,000. Caregivers are selected from the community, trained, and paid a small monthly sum by the government and a small fee by the parents of each child. Each caregiver takes care of six to eight children in her own home. The government provides loans for home improvement and donates toys and other necessities. Although financed by the government, the program is run by Fundación el Niño and other NGOs.

To complement the education interventions, Venezuela's Social Development Project will expand immunizations, preventive health care for infants, and treatment of acute diarrheal illness and respiratory infections among infants and children. It will also provide nutritional supplements to pregnant and lactating women and to children up to the age of six. Malnourished children will receive three kilograms of powdered whole milk a month, and all other children two kilograms. By the end of 1995 the project expects to have provided access to these basic services to 420,000 pregnant women (up from 200,000 in 1989), 360,000 lactating women (up from 80,000), 640,000 infants under age two (up from 245,000), and 916,000 children aged two to six (up from 370,000).

Informal and formal early child programs are now considered essential for improving conditions among the poor, and Venezuela will include them in the new structural adjustment program it is preparing in collaboration with the World Bank.

17. Tuning in to Learn about Child Care in the Philippines

The Philippines' village-based Parents Effectiveness Service was scoring real gains among parents—but it reached few. When people started tuning in to ECD School of the Air *and* The Filipino Family on the Air, *however, the audience for information on parenting and child care almost instantly grew by the thousands.*

The Philippines' village-based Parents Effectiveness Service (PER) has been teaching parents about early child development in group discussions and home visits since 1989. Its efforts seem to be paying off: parents participating in the program show a better grasp of what infants and young children need, both physically and for their mental development, and are consequently more encouraging and less violent toward them. But only a few parents were getting the message.

Then, in 1992, PER introduced *ECD School of the Air,* an educational radio program, in the southern and largely Muslim province of Mindanao. A series of 180 lessons were delivered over the air in three and a half months. Participating parents answered questions about the program in test booklets so that their progress could be monitored. By 1994, 10,500 parents had taken part in the *ECD School of the Air,* and even more were listening to *The Filipino Family on the Air,* a thirty-minute radio magazine show initiated in 1993 to run for thirteen weeks each season. Already reaching an estimated 80 percent of Filipino households, even in far-flung areas, radio can be a cost-effective, powerful medium for teaching parents how to give their children a better start in life—and PER is tapping that potential.

Box 13 UNICEF's video-based approach to parental education

Recognizing the mass media's great potential as an educational tool, UNICEF is sponsoring a program to produce videos and other mass media materials for use in its ongoing programs in early child development. In an effort supported by the UNICEF Global Education Fund, these teaching videos will first be tested in parental education projects in Iraq, Jordan, Morocco, Turkey, Tunisia, and Gaza and the West Bank and then adapted for use throughout the Middle East and North Africa.

For parents, UNICEF has produced a four-part videocassette series of TV-broadcast quality—with accompanying print materials—to convey the best strategies now known for encouraging young children's growth and development. The goal is to instruct 80 percent of parents in the Middle East and North Africa by the year 2000 in the basics of child care and development. If successful in that region, the videos will be distributed in other regions.

Under the direction of Dr. Cassie Landers, UNICEF's New York office has developed a core set of materials to convey the universal principles of early child development, incorporating existing materials whenever possible. These materials will be used as the basis for country-specific initiatives. Four ten-minute animated videos and accompanying guidebooks ("Off to a Good Start: The First Year of Life"; "A Time of Adventure: One- and Two-Year-Olds"; "Pathways to Learning: Three- and Four-Year-Olds"; "Ready for School: Five- and Six-Year-Olds") portray the normal sequence of a child's development, describing the major developmental tasks for each age group and showing how to create an effective learning environment in the home. To make the videos universally useful, realistic figures appear against neutral backgrounds. The animated series can be used with live-action sequences suited to the country setting or as stand-alone educational tools.

To produce videos in the countries where they are to be used, country teams are being formed of representatives from community NGOs; specialists in early education, nutrition, pediatrics, psychology, curriculum development, and training; video production and television specialists; and representatives from ministries of health, education, and social welfare. These groups are then divided into five working groups: concept design and development, video production, guidebooks and support materials, television broadcast, and community activities. Each working group consists of two to three people, and team members can serve on more than one to ensure continuity. The country teams work closely with UNICEF's New York office, which provides a timeline of tasks to be accomplished by each working group. UNICEF regional offices are responsible for coordinating and managing activity in the countries and communications with New York.

Source: From materials provided by Judith L. Evans, Consultative Group on Early Childhood Care and Development.

18. Using Radio to Teach Caregivers and Kids in Bolivia

In Bolivia an interactive radio program designed for use with young children in day care centers teaches children while also teaching the teachers—on how to interact with children and how to facilitate their development.

Bolivia is using an interactive radio program, *Jugando en el PIDI*, to teach children under six who attend Programa Integrado por Desarrollo Infantil (PIDI) centers, and at the same time to foster productive interaction between children and caregivers. Developed in 1993, the PIDI program seeks to use radio programs and cassettes as a cost-effective way to train teachers in developmentally appropriate techniques. The government agency Organismo Nacional del Menor, Mujer, y Familia is presently developing PIDI centers in the cities of El Alto, Santa Cruz, and Tarija.

For the pilot phase of the PIDI program, forty twenty-minute radio programs were designed around developmentally appropriate objectives for children aged three and four, to improve teachers' understanding of child development and of the activities best suited to each developmental stage. The programs were tested and extensively evaluated in 1993–94. The evaluations of the pilot series of *Jugando en el PIDI* found that it reflects the child development perspective, curriculum, and activities of the PIDI project by using active learning techniques, emphasizing the importance of learning environments, parents, and community, and providing interactive teacher training. The evaluations also provided continual feedback on the technical quality and pedagogical effectiveness of the programs, used in revising later programs.

Jugando en el PIDI includes stories on the adventures of Don Pancho and Katy, what Tía Clara has in her surprise bag, and the antics of the parrot Ito. Along with new material to be learned, it broadcasts catchy songs (which the children learn quickly), jokes, and activities.

Evaluators concluded that radio programs such as *Jugando en el PIDI* are a cheap and effective way to train both caregivers, many of whom are uneducated and illiterate, and early child program supervisors, who are frequently too ill-trained themselves to offer helpful advice. By reinforcing each new technique with hands-on experience, interactive radio helped teachers in the pilot program to learn new practices thoroughly and provided a framework around which teachers could organize PIDI program activities. The program also made children more active and alert. Evaluators found that children arriving at the PIDI centers are generally reticent, shy, passive, and nonverbal. Once educated with *Jugando en el PIDI* techniques, they become more active learners—and therefore far more disruptive in class. To help teachers learn how to channel the children's activity into productive avenues, set limits, and instill expectations for appropriate behavior, it was suggested that the teachers' guide, supervisors, and group meetings address the problem of classroom management more fully. Finally, evaluators remarked that *Jugando en el PIDI* was fun, and that teachers and children alike looked forward to the radio show with enthusiasm. For that reason, the program is very likely to continue to be useful.

19. Producing TV for Tots in Nigeria

With too little money to provide traditional preschool classrooms for all of its young children, Nigeria, assisted by the World Bank, is turning to educational television as a way to reach millions at relatively little cost.

Although Nigeria's national education policy seeks to improve educational opportunities for very young children, the country cannot afford to fund a traditional program for all of its 13 million preschoolers. The Nigeria Development Communications Project therefore proposes using the mass media—and the *Sesame Street* model—to teach children aged three to six and instruct their caregivers in active learning techniques.

The five-year pilot project will design, produce, disseminate, and evaluate mass media instructional materials for preschoolers and their mothers. To accomplish this, it will support the development of institutions to produce educational television materials and train television managers and evaluators. Its goal is to reach 4 million preschoolers, 36 percent of whom already have access to television. To broaden access, fifteen local government authorities in ten states have agreed to supply additional televisions for child care centers, and televisions will also be bought with the project and grant funding.

The instructional videos will not only be transmitted over the national network; they can also be shown from "video on wheels" vehicles and at local viewing centers. The newly established educational television unit of the Nigerian Television Authority plans to produce 130 episodes for preschool children, designed to develop their language expression and comprehension skills, their ability to observe and to solve problems, and their prenumeracy, preliteracy, and social skills. The shows will also convey basic health and hygiene information to parents.

In addition to the videos for children and parents, the project will prepare four to six videos for preschool organizers, facilitators, and trainers to show them how to identify children's basic needs, how best to organize available space, how to monitor children's health, how to create an environment for learning and for stimulating children's play, thinking, and expression, and how to make sure children are getting affection and good nutrition. Other videos will show parents how to observe the effects of children's interaction with adults and what children learn from such interaction.

The five-year pilot project, whose total cost is estimated at US$10.23 million, will be supported by an IDA credit of US$8.03 million, a Nigerian Television Authority grant of US$1.71 million, and a combined UNICEF and Bernard van Leer Foundation grant of US$490,000.

The Nigeria Development Communications Project will establish a new, collaborative way to produce educational videos in developing countries. Training sessions for this enterprise will include not only TV producers and scriptwriters, but also sociologists and early child development specialists. To evaluate the project's impact, baseline data on educational and social indicators are already being collected on children and adults in the targeted areas, and changes in these indicators will be monitored throughout the project.

If the Nigerian venture works, it could introduce an inexpensive and highly effective method for improving conditions for young children. As *Sesame Street* has shown in the United States, nothing is more powerful than TV for getting out the education message.

Bibliography

Atkin, Lucille. 1989. *Analysis of Instruments Used in Latin America to Measure Psychosocial Development in Children from 0 to 6 Years of Age.* Consultative Group on Early Child Development. New York: UNICEF House.

Bassett, Libby. 1985. *A Head Start: Preschool Education in Turkey.* International Development Research Center Report 14. Ottawa, Canada.

Bennett, John. 1993. "Early Childhood Care and Education Today—Worldwide Trends." In Lillian Katz, ed., *International Encyclopedia of Education.* 2d ed. New York: Pergamon.

Berg, Alan. 1987. *Malnutrition: What Can Be Done? Lessons from World Bank Experience.* Baltimore: Johns Hopkins University Press.

Bernard van Leer Foundation. 1994. *Why Children Matter: Investing in Early Childhood Care and Development.* The Hague.

Berrueta, Clement, Lawrence Schweinhart, Steve Barnett, A. Epstein, and David Weikart. 1984. *Changed Lives: The Effects of the Perry Preschool Program on Youths through 19.* Ypsilanti, Mich.: High/Scope Press.

Bloom, B.S. 1964. *Stability and Change in Human Characteristics.* New York: John Wiley & Sons.

Brazil, Ministry of Health, National Institute of Food and Nutrition. 1983. "Analização do PROAPE/Alagoas com Enfoque na Area Economica." Brasilia.

Campbell, Frances, and Craig T. Ramey. 1994. "Effects of Early Intervention on Intellectual and Academic Achievement: A Follow-up Study of Children from Low-Income Families." *Child Development* 65:684–98.

Carnegie Task Force on Meeting the Needs of Young Children. 1994. *Starting Points: Meeting the Needs of Our Youngest Children.* New York: Carnegie Corporation of New York.

Chaturvedi, E., B.C. Srivastava, J.V. Singh, and M. Prasad. 1987. "Impact of Six Years' Exposure to the ICDS Scheme on Psychosocial Development." *Indian Pediatrics* 24:153–64.

Chavez, A., H. Martinez, L. Allen, and G.H. Pelto. 1987. "The Collaborative Research and Support Program on Food Intake and Human Function: Mexico Project, Final Report." Report prepared for U.S. Agency for International Development, Washington, D.C.

Childcare Employee Project. 1992. "The National Childcare Staffing Study: Highlights of Major Findings and Recommendations." Oakland, Calif.

Children's Defense Fund. 1993. *Questions and Answers on Head Start.* Washington, D.C.

CINDE (International Center for Education and Human Development). 1990. "Highlights of an Evaluation of Project Promesa." CINDE-USA, Fort Lauderdale, Fla. Draft.

Clarke-Stewart, K.A. 1988. "The Effects of Infant Day Care Reconsidered." *Early Childhood Research Quarterly* 3:293–308.

Collins, Raymond C., and others. 1990. "Head Start Research and Evaluation: A Blueprint for the Future." Recommendations for the Advisory Panel for Head Start Evaluation Design Project. Collins Management Consulting, Vienna, Va.

Consultative Group on Early Childhood Care and Development. 1992. "Creating Linkages: Women, Work, and Child Care." *The Coordinators' Notebook* no. 11 (July). Haydenville, Mass.

———. 1993. "Health and Learning." *The Coordinators' Notebook* no. 13. Haydenville, Mass.

Donohue-Colletta, Nancy, ed. 1992. *Understanding Cross-Cultural Child Development and Designing Programs for Children.* New York: Christian Children's Fund.

Evans, Judith. 1995. "Who Is Caring for the Children? An Exploratory Survey Conducted in Hungary, Poland, Bulgaria and Romania, Part I: Main Report." Study for Consultative Group on Early Childhood Care and Development, Haydenville, Mass.

Feijo, M. 1984. "Early Childhood Education Programs and Children's Subsequent Learning: A Brazilian Case." Ph.D. dissertation. Stanford University, Department of Education, Stanford, Calif.

GAO (U.S. General Accounting Office). 1992. *Early Intervention: Federal Investments Like WIC Can Produce Savings.* GAO/HRD-92-18. Washington, D.C.

Gotts, Edward Earl. 1989. *HOPE, Preschool to Graduation: Contributions to Parenting and School-Family Relations Theory and Practice.* Charleston, W.Va.: Appalachia Educational Laboratory.

Grantham-McGregor, S.M., C.A. Powell, S.P. Walker, and J.H. Himes. 1991. "Nutritional Supplementation, Psychosocial Stimulation, and Mental Development of Stunted Children: The Jamaica Study." *Lancet* 338:1–5.

Gray, S.W., B.K. Ramsey, and R.A. Klaus. 1982. *From 3 to 20: The Early Training Project.* Baltimore: University Park Press.

Helburn, Suzanne, Mary L. Culkin, and others. 1995. "Cost, Quality, and Child Outcomes in Child Care Centers: Executive Summary." University of Colorado at Denver.

Herrera, M., and C. Super. 1983. "School Performance and Physical Growth of Underprivileged Children: Results of the Bogota Project at Seven Years." Report prepared for the World Bank, Washington, D.C. Harvard School of Public Health, Cambridge, Mass.

Hicks, L., R. Langham, and J. Takenaka. 1992. "Cognitive and Social Measures Following Early Nutritional Supplementation: A Sibling Study." *American Journal of Public Health* 72:1110–18.

Hohmann, Mary, and David P. Weikart. 1995. *Educating Young Children: Active Learning Practices for Preschool and Child Care Programs.* Ypsilanti, Mich.: High/Scope Education Research Foundation.

ICBF (Instituto Colombiano de Bienestar Familia). 1994. "Censo de Hogares Comunitarios de Bienestar de 0–8 años y Asociaciones de Padres de Familia: Resultados Preliminares." Santafé de Bogotá.

India, Department of Women and Children. 1988. *ICDS Scheme.* Delhi.

Infant Health and Development Program. 1990. "Enhancing the Outcomes of Low Birth Weight, Premature Infants: A Multisite Randomized Trial." *Journal of the American Medical Association* 263:3035–42.

Irvine, David. 1982. "Evaluation of the New York State Experimental Pre-Kindergarten Program." Paper presented at annual meeting of American Educational Research Association, New York.

Jones, Jean Yavis, and Joe Richardson. 1995. "Child Nutrition Programs: Facts and Issues." Congressional Research Service Report for Congress. Washington, D.C.

Kagitcibasi, Cigdem, D. Sunar, and S. Bekman. 1988. "Comprehensive Preschool Education Project: Final Report." Bogazici University, International Development Research Centre, Istanbul, Turkey.

Kajeckas, Margaret. 1995. "Head Start and WIC: How They Work and the Lessons They Hold for Developing Countries." World Bank, Human Development Department, Washington, D.C.

Katz, Lillian G. 1992. "Early Childhood Programs: Multiple Perspectives on Quality." *Childhood Education* 69(2):66.

Kirschner Associates. 1970. "A National Survey of the Impacts of Head Start Centers on Community Institutions." Albuquerque, N.M.

Klein, R. 1979. "Malnutrition and Human Behavior: A Backward Glance at an Ongoing Longitudinal Study." In D. Levitsky, ed., *Malnutrition, Environment and Behavior.* Ithaca, N.Y.: Cornell University Press.

Kresh, E. 1993. "The Effects of Head Start: What Do We Know?" Administration for Children and Families, Washington, D.C.

Lal, Sunder, and Raj Wati. 1986. "Non-Formal Preschool Education—An Effort to Enhance School Enrollment." Paper presented at National Conference on Research on Integrated Child Development Services, National Institute for Public Cooperation in Child Development (NIPCCD), New Delhi, February 25–29.

Lally, J.R., and others. 1987. "The Syracuse University Family Development Research Program: Long-Range Impact of an Early Intervention with Low-Income Children and Their Families." Far West Laboratory for Educational Research and Development, Center for Child and Family Studies, San Francisco.

Landers, Cassie, and Cigdem Kagitcibasi. 1990. "Measuring the Psychosocial Development of Young Children." Paper presented at Innocenti Technical Workshop, UNICEF International Child Development Centre, Florence, Italy, May 7–10.

Lazar, I., and R. Darlington. 1982. *Lasting Effects of Early Education: A Report from the Consortium for Longitudinal Studies.* Monographs of the Society for Research in Child Development 47 (Serial no. 195). Chicago: University of Chicago Press.

LeVine, R., S. Levine, A. Richman, F. Uribe, and C. Correa. 1994. "Schooling and Survival: The Impact of Maternal Education on Health Reproduction in the Third World." In L. Chen, A. Kleinman, and N. Ware, eds., *Health and Social Change: An International Perspective.* Boston: Harvard School of Public Health.

Levinger, Beryl. 1994. *Nutrition, Health, and Education for All.* Newton, Mass.: Education Development Center.

Levinger, Beryl, and Cornelia Janke. 1995. "Policies, Programs and Service Needs of Children: Implications for Project Design." Paper prepared for World Bank, Washington, D.C. Education Development Center, Newton, Mass.

Lewis, Catherine. 1995. *Educating Hearts and Minds: Reflections on Japanese Preschools.* New York: Cambridge University Press.

Lombard, Avima D. 1994. *Success Begins at Home: The Past, Present, and Future of the Home Instruction Program for Preschool Youngsters.* 2d ed. Guilford, Conn.: Dushkin Publishing Group.

Mathematica Policy Research. 1990. "The Savings in Medicaid Costs for Newborns and Their Mothers from Prenatal Participation in the WIC Program." Report prepared for U.S. Department of Agriculture, Office of Analysis and Evaluation, Washington, D.C.

———. 1991. "The Savings in Medicaid Costs for Newborns and Their Mothers from Prenatal Participation in the WIC Program: Addendum." Report prepared for U.S. Department of Agriculture, Office of Analysis and Evaluation, Washington, D.C.

———. 1992. "Very Low Birthweight among Medicaid Newborns in Five States: The Effects of Prenatal WIC Participation." Report prepared for U.S. Department of Agriculture, Office of Analysis and Evaluation, Washington, D.C.

———. 1993. "Infant Mortality among Medicaid Newborns in Five States: Effects of Prenatal WIC Participation." Report prepared for U.S. Department of Agriculture, Office of Analysis and Evaluation, Washington, D.C.

McCall, Robert B. 1993. "Head Start: Its Potential, Its Achievements, Its Future." University of Pittsburgh Center for Social and Urban Research, Pittsburgh, Penn.

McCormick, Marie. 1985. "The Contribution of Low Birth Weight to Infant Mortality and Childhood Morbidity." *New England Journal of Medicine* 312:82–90.

McKay, A. 1982. "Longitudinal Study of the Long-term Effects of the Duration of Early Childhood Intervention on Cognitive Ability and Primary School Performance." Ph.D. dissertation. Northwestern University, Evanston, Ill.

McKay, R.H., L. Condelli, H. Ganson, B.J. Barnett, C. McCouley, and M.C. Plantz. 1985. *The Impact of Head Start on Children, Families and Communities: Final Report of the Head Start Evaluation, Synthesis and Utilization Project.* Washington, D.C.: U.S. Department of Health and Human Services.

Midco Educational Associates. 1972. "Investigation of the Effects of Parent Participation in Head Start." Report to the Office of Child Development, Denver, Colo.

Mitchell, Anne, Heather Weiss, and Tom Schultz. 1992. "Evaluating Education Reform: Early Childhood Education." Paper prepared for U.S. Department of Education, Office of Educational Research and Improvement, Washington, D.C.

Monroe, E., and M.S. McDonald. 1981. "A Follow-up of the 1966 Head Start Program." Rome City Schools, Rome, Ga.

Myers, Robert. 1990. *Toward a Fair Start for Children: Programming for Early Childhood Care and Development in the Developing World.* Paris: UNESCO.

———. 1995. *The Twelve Who Survive: Strengthening Programs of Early Childhood Development in the Third World.* 2d ed. Ypsilanti, Mich.: High/Scope Press.

Myers, Robert, and others. 1985. "Preschool Education as a Catalyst for Community Development." Report prepared for U.S. Agency for International Development, Lima, Peru.

Nimnicht, G., and P.E. Posada. 1986. "The Intellectual Development of Children in Project Promesa." Research and Evaluation Report 1. Report prepared for Bernard van Leer Foundation. Centro International de Educación y Desarrollo Humano (CINDE), Medellin, Colombia.

NIPCCD (National Institute of Public Cooperation and Child Development). 1992. *National Evaluation of Integrated Child Development Services.* New Delhi.

Osborn, A.F., and J.E. Milbank. 1987. *The Effects of Early Education: A Report from the Child Health and Education Study.* New York: Oxford University Press.

Palmer, F. 1983. "The Harlem Study: Effects by Type of Training, Age of Training and Social Class." In Consortium for Longitudinal Studies, ed., *As the Twig Is Bent: Lasting Effects of Preschool Programs.* Hillsdale, N.J.: Lawrence Earlbaum.

Parker, F.L., and others. 1987. "Head Start as a Social Support for Mothers: The Psychological Benefits of Involvement." *American Journal of Orthopsychiatry* 57(2):220–23.

Pollitt, Ernesto, and E. Metallinos-Katsaras. 1990. "Iron Deficiency and Behavior: Constructs, Methods and Validity of the Findings." In

Richard Wurtman and Judith Wurtman, eds., *Nutrition and the Brain*, vol. 8, *Behavioral Effects of Metals, and Their Biochemical Mechanisms.* New York: Raven.

Powell, C., and S. Grantham-McGregor. 1989. "Home Visiting of Varying Frequency and Child Development." *Pediatrics* 84:157–64.

Price, H.R., E.L. Cowen, R.P. Lorion, and J. Ramos-McKay, eds. 1988. *14 Ounces of Prevention.* Washington, D.C.: American Psychological Association.

Psacharopoulos, George. 1982. "The Economics of Early Childhood Services: A Conceptual Framework and Some Empirical Dimensions." In *Caring for Young Children: An Analysis of Educational and Social Services.* Paris: Organization for Economic Cooperation and Development, Center for Educational Research and Innovation.

———. 1986. "Returns to Education: A Further International Update and Implications." *Journal of Human Resources* 20:583–601.

Ramey, C.T., D.M. Bryant, F.A. Campbell, J.J. Sparling, and B.H. Wassik. 1988. "Early Intervention for High-Risk Children: The Carolina Early Intervention Program." In H.R. Price, E.L. Cowen, R.P. Lorion, and J. Ramos-McKay, eds., *14 ounces of Prevention.* Washington, D.C.: American Psychological Association.

Ramey, C.T., K.O. Yeates, and E.J. Short. 1984. "The Placticity of Intellectual Development: Insights from Prevention Intervention." *Child Development* 55:1913–25.

Ramey, C.T., and others. 1990. "Early Intervention: Why, for Whom, How and at What Cost?" *Clinics in Perinatology* 17:47–55.

Ramey, S.L., and C.T. Ramey. 1992. "Early Educational Intervention with Disadvantaged Children—To What Effect?" *Applied and Preventive Psychology* 1:131–40.

Richards, H. 1985. *The Evaluation of Cultural Action.* London: Macmillan.

Roopnarine, J.L., and J.E. Johnson, eds. 1993. *Approaches to Early Child Education.* New York: Macmillan.

Rush, David, and others. 1988. "The National WIC Evaluation: Evaluation of the Special Supplemental Food Program for Women, Infants, and Children." *American Journal of Clinical Nutrition,* supplement, 48(2).

Save the Children Foundation. 1995. "Strong Beginnings." Westport, Conn.

Schweinhart, Lawrence J. 1992. "Early Child Education." In Marvin C. Alkin, ed., *Encyclopedia of Educational Research.* 6th ed. New York: Pergamon.

Schweinhart, Lawrence J., Helen V. Barnes, and David P. Weikart. 1993. *Significant Benefits: The High/Scope Perry Preschool Study through Age 27.* Monographs of High/Scope Educational Research Foundation 10. Ypsilanti, Mich.: High/Scope Press.

Schweinhart, Lawrence J., and David P. Weikart. 1980. *Young Children Grow Up: The Effects of the Perry Preschool Program on Youths through Age 15.* Ypsilanti, Mich.: High/Scope Press.

———. 1983. "The Effects of Perry Preschool on Youths through Age 15." In Consortium for Longitudinal Studies, ed., *As the Twig Is Bent: Lasting Effects of Preschool Programs.* Hillsdale, N.J.: Lawrence Earlbaum.

Selowsky, M. 1981. "Nutrition, Health, and Education: The Economic Significance of Complementarities at Early Age." *Journal of Developmental Economics* 9:331–46.

Swaminathan, M. 1990. *The First Three Years: A Sourcebook on Early Childhood Care and Education.* Report ED-90/WS-28, UNESCO-UNICEF Cooperative Programme Digest, number 31. Paris.

UNESCO. 1991. *International Directory on the Young Child and the Family Environment.* Paris.

———. 1992. *Directory of Early Childhood Care and Education Organizations in Sub-Saharan Africa.* Paris.

UNESCO and Bernard van Leer Foundation. 1995. *Enhancing the Skills of Early Childhood Trainers.* Paris: UNESCO.

UNESCO, YCFE (Young Child and the Family Environment) Project. 1995. *International Directory of Early Childhood Care.* Paris: UNESCO.

UNICEF. 1993. *Towards a Comprehensive Strategy for the Development of the Young Child: An Inter-Agency Policy Review.* New York: UNICEF House.

———. 1994. *Women and Gender in Countries in Transition: A UNICEF Perspective.* UNICEF Regional Office for Central and Eastern Europe and Commonwealth of Independent and Baltic States. Florence, Italy.

———. 1995. "Summary Report of ICDC Workshop on Early Childhood Development Policy Update." Presented at International Child Development Center workshop on Early Child Development Policy, Innocenti Child Development Center, June 1–7. New York.

U.S. Department of Agriculture, Food and Nutrition Service. 1994. "Special Supplemental Nutrition Program for Women, Infants and Children Regulations." 7 CFR, part 246 et. seq. Washington, D.C.

Wagner, D., and J. Spratt. 1987. "Cognitive Consequences of Contrasting Pedagogies: The Effects of Quaranic Pre-schooling in Morocco." *Child Development* 58:1209–19.

Wilson, Sandra. 1995. "ECD Programs: Lessons from Developing Countries." World Bank, Human Development Department, Washington, D.C.

World Bank. 1993. *World Development Report 1993: Investing in Health.* New York: Oxford University Press.

———. 1995. "Report on Second Tamil Nadu Integrated Nutrition Project." Operations Evaluation Department. Washington, D.C.

Yip, Ray. 1987. "Declining Prevalence of Anemia among Low-Income Children in the United States." *Journal of the American Medical Association* 258:1619–23.

Zigler, Edward, and Susan Muenchow. 1992. *Head Start: The Inside Story of America's Most Successful Educational Experiment.* New York: HarperCollins.

Zigler, Edward, and Sally J. Styfco. 1994. "Is the Perry Preschool Better Than Head Start? Yes and No." *Early Childhood Research Quarterly* 9:267–87.

Zigler, Edward, C. Taussig, and K. Black. 1992. "Early Childhood Intervention: A Promising Preventative for Juvenile Delinquency." *American Psychologist* 47:997–1006.